All the Sun Goes Round

Tales From the Zodiac

Reina James

The Wessex Astrologer

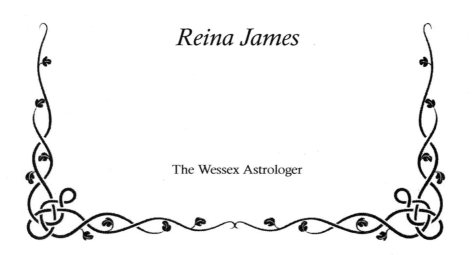

Published in 2010 by
The Wessex Astrologer Ltd
4A Woodside Road
Bournemouth
BH5 2AZ
England

www.wessexastrologer.com

ISBN 9781902405490

A catalogue record of this book is available at The British Library

Cover design by Dave at Creative Byte, Poole, Dorset

Printed in Great Britain by the MPG Books Group, Bodmin and King's Lynn

For Mike

With Love

I'd love these tales to capture your imagination so much that you end up reading them all. You may well find that several resonate more strongly with you than your own sun sign. There are many astrological reasons for this and I hope that this book will encourage some of you to investigate your individual birth charts more closely.

Every character and creature here reflects something of the sign it represents. There are no goodies or baddies; we're all capable of achieving wonders and being disagreeable in the very same breath. But if you think I might be describing an aspect of you that you'd sooner pin on somebody else, forgive me.

Contents

ARIES   Flame Davey   1

TAURUS   The Empress   11

GEMINI   Cissy and Sem   21

CANCER   Thomas Coates   31

LEO   The King   41

VIRGO   Kate   51

LIBRA   Mr Spoons   61

SCORPIO   Absalee   71

SAGITTARIUS   Jack Fortune   81

CAPRICORN   Anwen   91

AQUARIUS   William Crane   101

PISCES   Meggie Mary   109

Aries
Flame Davey

lame Davey was forbidden to go out alone, even though he was twelve years old and nearly as strong as his father. When he was a very small boy, the town he lived in had been besieged. A terrible creature with a roomy jaw and eyes like raw liver had come stamping and roaring down the main street, its great arms stretched out to lift and kill.

For the first few days there was panic. The creature was hungry and came to the town at all hours, crashing through doors and gardens and sweeping children and animals into its mouth. Then it started to visit in the afternoons, just as the children were coming home from school, so the school day was changed but the creature found them and killed them just the same. After a while, when its stores were full, the raids became more haphazard and sometimes a week passed, even two, without a death; not that that was any consolation to the slaughtered.

When Flame Davey was three, the creature took his mother. He was in his father's arms when they came across it, half in and half out of the house, with her in its grip. Ewan had covered the boy's face with his hand and waited, still as a mountain, while the creature turned and thundered home. That night, he tried to persuade the people of the town that they should fight back. 'It'll kill us all!' he shouted. 'Why don't we follow it tomorrow and find out where it lives, then we can trap it and set fire to its lair!'

'You must be mad!' someone shouted back. 'You're raving because you've lost your wife,' said another. 'Do you want Davey to grow up without a father too?' So the people hid from danger and cursed the creature and the only battles they fought were with each other.

Flame Davey saw his father trudging down the street and ran down the stairs to meet him at the door. 'Did you kill it today? Did you cut its head off?'

'No, Davey, not today.' Ewan put down his sword and took off his bloody clothes. While he washed and put ointment on the worst cuts and bruises, Davey lit a fire and made supper.

'Tell me what happened today, tell me now,' said the boy, his eyes bright, his hair so red that it looked hot on his head.

'I did my best to get near the cave,' said Ewan, 'But the creature was watching, the way it sometimes does, from behind a tree or a wall.'

'One day you'll kill it. One day they'll know you saved the town and we'll all be happy then won't we, when it's gone?'

'Yes, sweet boy, we will,' said Ewan, flinching as he pulled on his clean shirt. 'We certainly will.'

'And what happened today? When it smelt you out?'

'Oh, I crept up to it when it was busy scratching and stabbed it in the leg!'

'What did it do?'

'It was so angry I thought its eyes would roast in their sockets! Then it kicked out and caught me with its foot, or I might have got in closer.'

'I think you'll kill it tomorrow. I know it'll be soon!'

That night, Ewan lay awake for a long time, thinking of Davey's mother and her poppy-red hair.

To fool the creature, the children had started going to school at odd hours, no day the same as the day before. Apart from finishing his homework, Davey was free to do as he wished until the afternoon. When Ewan had gone, he sat at the table, banging the lid on his pencil box. Soon, he would get a sword of his own and join Ewan at the lair...

A pinprick of light caught his eye. He moved his head, seeking it out. The light glinted again, like a star flickering in his father's bed. Puzzled, he got up and pulled at the muddle of blankets. And there, its blade flaring on the dark wool, was Ewan's sword.

Davey picked it up and ran down to the street, even though he'd been told a hundred times that he wasn't to go out by himself. How could he let his father fight the creature bare-handed? The sword was heavy and hindered him but Ewan had been slower still and soon Davey caught sight of him in the distance, walking with his head held low.

Davey quickened his pace and was about to call out when Ewan stopped abruptly, wiped his hand across his mouth, turned and left the road. He headed for a dark archway and then passed through into the street beyond. This wasn't the way to the creature! Taken aback, Davey arrived at the turning and peered round the corner. A ratty man with a bottle in his hand was offering Ewan a leather bag. Ewan took the bag, refused a drink from the bottle and walked away into the worming streets. The man laughed and followed, slapping him on the shoulder.

Davey pursued them, more curious than afraid, until they came to a cobbled square where a gang of men was building a platform, knocking stakes in at each corner and linking them with lengths of rope. The ratty man looked at the crowd that was gathering and scratched his ear with a stick that he'd picked up from the cobbles. Ewan slipped into an alley, bag in hand, and was lost to view. Davey couldn't go after him without crossing the square and giving himself away so he knelt down by a low wall and waited, his muscles taut with the need to take action. He had the sword. He could help. The more he thought about it, the more he wanted to let his father know that he was there.

Ewan appeared at the mouth of the alley. Davey got up, ready to reveal himself but the words froze in his mouth. His father was pulling on a black hood. His bruised chest was bare and his feet without shoes. He walked towards the ring and Davey followed, standing behind the crowd with the sword held at his back, more frightened than he had ever been in his life.

The ratty man got under the ropes and jumped onto the platform. He found the sturdiest stake and leant on it with one elbow. 'I see you found us then!' he shouted. 'And we'll be having you up here nice and quick before that creature comes looking!' The men mumbled and shuffled, eager and embarrassed at once. He pointed down at Ewan who was standing on the cobbles with his head lowered and his arms folded across his chest.

'Here he is! The man you love to hate! The man you love to fight! The man you love to beat! *The Hammer*!' People jeered and waved their fists as Ewan climbed into the ring. He snatched off his hood and growled at the crowd like an angry dog. 'Who'll give me copper to win gold?' said the ratty man. 'Who'll be the first to fight?'

One by one, men from the crowd came up to the platform. Sometimes Ewan was beaten to the floor and then Davey held the sword to his shivering body and wept. Sometimes Ewan won with a single punch and danced round the ring with his arms high, provoking the crowd and then, despite himself, Davey wanted to yell, 'The Hammer's my father! You watch out!'

Between the bouts he stayed still, too frightened to move. As soon as the fighting was over, he crept away and dragged himself home.

He sat by the cold grate, waiting. When Ewan came into the room, Davey clamped his teeth tight shut and balled his hands into fists.

'Are you alright, sweet boy?' said Ewan, reaching out for a welcome.

Davey shook him off. 'You left this behind,' he said. He got up and lifted the sword from his father's bedclothes. 'Weren't you scared, not having it?'

'I managed,' said Ewan. 'I dug a pit and tried to trick him into it.'

'Like you tricked me.'

'I've never tricked you. You're my life, my own boy. Why would I do that to you?'

'I followed you today and you walked past me and didn't even know I was there.' Tears poured down Davey's face and he wiped at them angrily. 'And you're not fighting the creature at all! You're stupid and I hate you!' He kicked the table leg and stood facing Ewan, his face ugly with rage.

'How dare you go out alone!' shouted Ewan. 'You might have been taken! You might have been killed!'

They stared at each other, terrified. Davey was the first to move. He walked past his father to the fireplace, put the sword carefully on the hearth and sat at the table, pretending to do his homework. 'You lied,' he said, making a great show of finding the right page in his book.

'I didn't want to lie,' said Ewan, holding a hand out to Davey, who took no notice. 'And I did try to fight. At the beginning.'

'I don't care.'

Ewan didn't speak again, even to wish Davey goodnight. They both went to their beds in the dark, angry, helpless and very far apart.

Davey lay curled up in a ball, his hair just visible, copper-red wires on the pillow. When his father got up he lay so still that it hurt him to breathe. He heard some noise in the corner of the room where they kept food and plates, then, 'Oh, what's the use!' as Ewan cut himself and threw the bread he was slicing onto the floor. There was more noise as Ewan tried to find something to wipe the blood from his hand, then a moment of silence, then the bang of the door closing. Davey was alone.

He stretched his legs, pleased to be able to move. His homework lay unfinished on the table. He didn't want to open his books; he wasn't allowed to go out and he didn't want to stay in. Thinking that he might as well be warm while he made up his mind what to do, he got dressed, went to the wood basket for logs and kindling and took an armful to the hearth.

The sword had gone. He dropped the wood onto the floor, ran to his father's bed and pulled off all the blankets. The bed was empty. The sword was nowhere in the room: not under the furniture, not in the cupboards, not even outside the door. He ran to the window. Ewan was almost out of sight now, a spot of colour in the distance.

Was he truly going to fight the creature? Fumbling with his shoes, Davey flew down the stairs and ran after him.

As he got nearer he could see the sword clearly, hanging from Ewan's waist. But Ewan wasn't walking to the scrubland and the creature's lair. He was doing exactly what he'd done the day before, leaving the road for the gloomy archway.

'You're late,' said the ratty man, lifting a piece of greasy meat in one hand and a bottle in the other. 'I thought you weren't coming.'

'I was tired,' said Ewan. 'I nearly didn't. Let's get to work.'

Davey watched, confused, as his father walked away. Unable to move, to go home or to follow, he stood wretchedly in the shadows for many long minutes, with his hands in fists at his side. He wanted to fight the creature then and there, without a sword, just to prove that he wasn't like his father; he was brave!

By the time he reached the makeshift ring, the ratty man was shouting at the crowd, provoking them to fight. Ewan stood quietly to the side with his arms folded and the sword at his waist.

'...it's the man you love to hate, the Hammer!' As everyone moved in to watch the first bout, Davey was pushed to the front. He looked up and found his father staring down at him, his eyes glinting in the black hood.

'Hello, sweet boy,' whispered Ewan. 'Wait now.' He uncovered his face and held the sword up with a flourish, swinging it round his head..

'I'm not fighting him if he's using that thing!' said a man in the queue, but nobody laughed. Ewan dropped his arm and turned full circle in the ring, looking closely at every gawping face below.

'It's been too long, the way we live. I'm ashamed. My wife is dead and my boy here –', Ewan went to the rope and leant over to touch Davey's hair, '– my boy here has never known what it is to be safe. Will we not stop fighting each other? Will you come with me instead and fight the thing that gives us grief?'

The ratty man tried to get back into the ring but Ewan pushed him away and he fell clumsily into the crowd, legs flying. Nobody dared to speak. Then the ground shuddered, as if a fist was battering up at them from below. The creature was on the march. A series of crashes and screams broke in on the silence and the crowd began to fall away, anxious to get home.

'*Now!*' roared Ewan. He jumped down and ran towards the noise, so full of battle that he could think of nothing else, not even his son.

'Fight!' shouted Davey, jumping on the spot. 'Fight! Fight! Fight!' Some people took up the cry and ran to catch up with Ewan. Seeing a small army beginning to form, the more fearful took heart and straggled along behind. Soon everyone was leaving the square, chanting and waving debris that they'd found on the pavements.

Flame Davey was the last to leave. He climbed into the ring and stood listening to the creature as it snarled and thundered towards the mob. 'My dad's The Hammer,' he shouted, punching the air with both fists and imagining his father lifted high in triumph, 'So that's the end of you!'

Taurus

The Empress

he Empress tossed and turned on her goose down mattress. The pillows were soft and the sheets fine-spun but she might as well have been lying on boulders and barbed wire, so badly did the night pass. At eight o'clock sharp, just as she'd drifted off to sleep, her string quartet began to scratch out their musical alarm in the gardens below. She woke and stumbled out of bed. 'Go away!' she bellowed, slamming the window shut and clumping off to her morning bath.

The water was lukewarm and the last scrappy bit of soap fell to pieces as she washed, leaving tiny fragments that stuck to her skin. There were no towels. She called for her maid, Dora, who ran in with them and patted and soothed as best she could, but by now the Empress was in an inconsolable sulk, her bottom lip pushed out so far that it nearly touched her chin. While Dora dressed and perfumed her and plaited her hair into loops around her head, the Empress's mood went from bad to worse. 'This necklace is too tight,' she complained. 'And that soap's given me a rash and you smell horribly of onions.' As the last pin went into her hair, she tore off the necklace and threw it at the wall, cascading blue jewels over the carpet.

In the palace kitchen, the cook, who had gone to fetch the butter from the larder, slipped in a puddle of cream. Reaching out to save herself she dropped the dish, pulled four dozen fat brown eggs with her to the floor, bumped her head on a side of bacon, groaned, and fell into the muslin bags that were dripping curds for cheese. As she slithered to a stop, her left foot landed squarely in what was left of the sticky, eggy, yellow butter.

'Oh, pig's knees!' said the cook. The bell rang. The Empress was hungry for her breakfast. The cook scraped up what butter she could, worked it quickly into a little golden hen and put it on the laden tray.

The Empress smelt the egg before she saw it, cold and grey and wobbling on the plate. Pushing it away, she reached for a slice of toast but there was fluff in the butter and a dead thing in the jam; in a real temper now, she pulled on the bell rope until it came tumbling to the floor. After that there was a great deal of fuss made about breakfast. Thick pancakes were fried and served with fresh tea and the Empress ate steadily until all the plates were empty.

When she was full, she left the table, padded to the palace stairs and began to climb. Each flight was steeper and more narrow than the last but she struggled on, breathless and red in the face, with her hand pressed to the stitch in her side. On and on she climbed until she reached the very top floor where she rested, waiting for the shaking in her legs to stop.

Then, happy at last, she opened the first of the six big doors that lay ahead of her. The room was large and lined with shelves that were stacked from end to end with wooden boxes. She lifted the first box to the window and opened it as tenderly as she might have opened a love letter. Nestling in the centre, tucked into a satin pillow, was a plump, milky pearl, so perfect that it seemed to have trapped the moon in its skin. She held the pearl to her face and rolled it in her palms; then she threaded it onto a golden chain and put it round her neck. In the next box she found amber and gold and the next, silver set with opals and jade.

The Empress ran from box to box, putting rings on her fingers and rings on her toes and encircling her waist and neck with layer upon layer of every kind of jewel. She perched twinkling crowns on her hair, wrapped emeralds round her ankles and clutched what was left in her hands as she danced slowly round the room. When she'd had her fill of the jewels, she kissed each one and returned them all to their boxes, leaving only a sapphire bracelet wound about her arm.

The second door opened onto a room lined with mirrors and occupied by a tall wooden roundabout of dresses and robes in every possible shade of green and pink and blue. The morning's ordeals had made the Empress too cross with clothes to get undressed and dressed again so she chose a long cloak: a profusion of dried rose petals sewn onto lace so fine that at first glance the petals hung unsupported in the air. Holding the cloak over her shoulders, she glided from wall to wall to see her reflection in each of the four mirrors.

In the third room she uncorked small bottles of scent: walnut cake, clean sheets, ripe peaches and bracken.

In the fourth room she lay on a floor strewn with soft cushions and looked up at a canopy embroidered with thread that shone like stars, even in the darkest place.

The fifth room held wonders: a tiny shoe carved from an apple pip, a chair with hands that stroked her head if it was aching and a doll that stood up and gave her flowers, then tucked them away in its pocket, ready to give again.

The last room along the corridor, the sixth, was the most extraordinary of all. There was nothing special to see, only shelves lined with old brown clay jars, each topped with a wooden lid and sealed with wax. On a table next to the door lay a crystal the size and colour of a stick of rhubarb and beside it, a dog-eared book listing the contents of the jars. The Empress opened the book and made her choice.

As she reached up, spreading her fingers to take the chosen jar from the shelf, something furry crawled across her thumb. She shrieked. She examined her hand, looked up her sleeve, fetched the little ladder that allowed her access to the higher shelves and searched for vermin. There was nothing to be seen but dust and fluff. Tutting at her silliness, she took down the chosen jar and put it on the table. Then with one end of the crystal to her ear, she leant forwards and placed the other end on the belly of the pot. Music seeped through the clay and up into the crystal. Smiling, she closed her eyes.

Her scalp was prickling. She put her hand to her hair. There was a flutter and a buzz, and a creeping thing under her fingers. A bee was sitting on her head.

She screamed and the bee skedaddled and as the Empress turned this way and that, the jar went crashing to the hard stone floor and broke into a dozen pieces. As it fell open a choir of angel voices ricocheted round the walls, all but deafening the Empress, who stopped screaming and stood with her mouth open and tears spilling from her eyes. The music soared and died away, stretching out its long last notes, leaving a silence so empty that the room might well have been buried in deep earth.

The Empress picked up the largest broken fragment and pressed the crystal to it, willing the choir to have penetrated the clay. It was as mute as a soup plate. With a roar of disappointment she hurled it away from her and fixed her green eyes on the gap in the shelf. The bee, made brave by the stillness, crawled out, saw her terrible gaze and flew for its life. The Empress didn't see him. She was staring blindly, thinking that the choir would be scattered now, old and croaky, all magic gone. All the songs in the Empire had been trapped and kept in this room and new songs were rarely found, people being disinclined to have them taken away. How was the Empress to fill another jar?

There was only one place left in her lands to explore. A forbidden place; an absolutely out of the question, not even to be considered place.

The Empress went to dress for an afternoon out.

The Emperor, her father, had recognized quite early on in his reign that certain people, certain places, were not to be governed in an ordinary way. He also recognized that if you left these people and places to their own devices you could get on with pushing everyone else about and having quite a good time of it. Which is exactly what he did. As the years passed and the Emperor got older and became more ill humoured, the Certain people, as they had come to be known, began to gather in one small area. So he planted brambles around their lands and gave them a single gateway for access that they rarely bothered to use.

Then the Emperor went a little mad, perceived the Certain people to be a dreadful threat and stupidly decreed their lands to be out of bounds to all, especially his daughter. He never quite told her why she was forbidden to visit there, he hardly knew himself. But she had grown up believing it to be a terrible place and, until the calamity of the broken jar, had always observed her father's wishes.

As her coach neared the gateway in the bramble wall, the Empress sat up straight and set herself mutinously to the task.

'Do we have to, ma'am?' said the coachman, who was wishing that he'd taken up pig-farming like his brother.

'Get on with it!' said the Empress. 'And stop snivelling!'

Expecting nothing less than an unpleasant, possibly momentous journey, she was astonished by the dullness of the landscape. The trees were perhaps a little greener, the birds a little louder but the houses were ordinary enough and the people they glimpsed looked no different to anyone else in her empire. As they journeyed on, the Empress grew bolder and leant out of the window, straining to catch sight or sound of some strangeness in this simple place. But there was only a tedious road to follow and after an hour or so she grew bored and decided to go home.

Which is when she heard the voice.

Hissing at the coachman to stop, the Empress stepped down from the coach and stood in the road, listening. Whoever was making the sound was hidden from view by a tall hedge. Holding up her skirts, she climbed onto a large tree stump and looked over the boundary into a cottage garden. She saw a woman of her own age, working her way steadily along a row of raspberries, singing as she picked. The Empress gawped. No fruit in the palace had ever been so huge with juice, no roses so sweetly perfumed. She could have swooned and been carried on the scent! She thought of her dreary palace gardens, the miserable little blotches of colour, the puny flowers and the scabby apples...

The song was strange, unlike any in the jars, and the woman's voice was rich and dark, like the soil at her feet. Excited now, the Empress tried to leap off the tree stump but she caught her foot in her skirt, toppled headlong into the squelchy earth and staggered back to the coach, slapping at her dress and straightening her hat.

'Announce me!' she said. The coachman ran to the gate and threw it open with a flourish. 'Be upstanding,' he shouted, 'for the Empress of the Six Lands!'

The Certain woman looked up from the raspberries and smiled, as if strange, unruly people burst into her garden every afternoon.

'That song,' the Empress said at once. 'Is that what makes your garden grow?'

'Possibly,' said the woman. 'In fact I wouldn't be at all surprised.'

The Empress resolved to keep the upper hand. 'Your garden –' she started to say.

'Yes?' replied the woman, lifting a raspberry to her mouth and bending to pick another.

Overwhelmed by this impudence, the Empress shouted, 'You must come to the palace! I want you to sing in my garden. I want it to be beautiful, like yours.'

'I'll come if you're sure,' said the woman. 'But I can't answer for what might happen.'

'Come!' said the Empress, walking back to the gate.

'If you're sure...'

They sat as far apart as possible in the coach, each reluctant to be too close to the other. The coachman hadn't understood a word of what had passed between them but he drove the horses hard, anxious to be back in the safety of the stables. The Empress stared out of the window, seeing nothing. In her mind's eye she was introducing the woman and her song to the kitchen garden, aiming her at the flowerbeds, marching her through the orchards, the orangery and the vines. And what if she took her upstairs, to her treasures! What if there could be more of *everything*?

When they arrived at the palace, the Empress hurried the Certain woman into the great hall and ordered a servant to bring a jar, a lid and sealing wax. 'You'll sing your song into this,' said the Empress, pushing the jar at her face.

'If that's what you want,' said the woman. 'But the song –'

'Just sing!' said the Empress.

'You might –'

'Now!'

The Certain woman's voice found its way to every corner of the palace, bewitching the servants who came running and pushing at each other to get closer to the sound. As the Empress opened her mouth to send them about their business, she was suddenly distracted by a quiver of movement in her fingers. The jar was disappearing, spilling through them! She tried to catch it, but in seconds it was no more than a little heap of dry clay at her feet. Then the carpets began to shrink away like smoke and the chandeliers rained crystal dust and the long table rustled and shivered until it burst into a pepper-coloured cloud and set the servants screaming.

'Stop this!' the Empress bellowed, clutching a chair with both hands and willing it to stay whole, 'STOP!' But she didn't think to stop the song, and the chair, along with every other thing of beauty in the great hall, disintegrated as surely as if it had been powdered by a millstone. Half-mad with terror, she scrambled up the stairs, gulping and choking on the dry air, deaf to the pandemonium below and oblivious to the pain in her side, up and up and up she went, up to the silent passage and the six wooden doors.

When the song was over, the Certain woman looked about her and marvelled at the hills and valleys of dust. A noise, not quite like singing, not quite like crying, was drifting faintly down the stairs. Picking her way carefully over the floor, she climbed the many flights, humming as she went.

The Empress was kneeling on her powdered jewels, croaking what she could remember of the song. When she saw the woman, she struggled to her feet and grabbed her arm. 'Did you do this?' she said. 'Did you dare to do this? Put it all back! I order you!'

'It wasn't my song to give,' said the woman. 'And it wasn't yours to take.'

The Empress scooped up a handful of the dust and threw it at her. 'It's not fair,' she wailed, 'Your flowers, your fruit...'

Taking the Empress firmly by the hand, the Certain woman smiled. 'Come with me,' she said. And in the blush of early morning, they walked the long road home to her garden and picked raspberries together and ate them all for breakfast.

Gemini

Cissy and Sem

issy and Sem were sister and brother. They lived in a big-enough house in a small neighbourly village and shared most things between them except, as Cissy complained, the housework, the shopping and the cooking. She took care of those, not because she wanted to but because Sem never seemed to have the time.

One night after supper, Cissy was darning while Sem was sitting at the table, making a house of cards. 'I forgot to tell you,' she said, choosing a sock from the basket at her feet. 'I'm delivering the post tomorrow.'

Cleaves, the post master, was prone to nervous upsets which sent him fretfully to bed and Cissy had long since volunteered to be his deputy. 'I'll deliver some for you, if you don't give me too many,' said Sem, putting the last card on the house and sweeping the base away so that the cards fell all over the floor. He left them there and banged the table leg with his foot. 'Bet you don't know what a pack adds up to.'

'Ace as one?'

'If you like.'

'Three hundred and forty,' said Cissy, without a pause.

'Too slow.'

Cissy threw a pair of socks at his head. He caught them and put one on each hand to make a puppet show, with jokes so funny that she had to laugh, even though she didn't want to.

Cissy divided the post into two sacks. Sem was to go out to the farms while she delivered to the village, but by the time he'd done half the round he was bored. There were only a few parcels left, so he sat with his feet cooling in a brook and ate some small sweet carrots that he'd taken from a box by a farmer's gate. After that he lay down on the grass and fell deeply asleep. When he woke, the sun was low in the sky. For a moment he had no idea where he was, then he saw the sack of parcels. It was too late to do anything about it now; he'd miss supper and Cissy would be cross. Looking round to make sure he was alone, he emptied them all into the bushes.

'I'll come back tomorrow,' he said to himself, 'and deliver them before anybody notices.'

Cissy had finished her round before Sem had stolen the carrots and when he got home, waving his empty sack, she'd already made the supper and had some time to think. She put the plates on the table and sat watching him.

'What's to eat?' said Sem.

'Wash your hands,' said Cissy, sure that he hadn't.

'I delivered everything,' he said, 'so you don't have to worry about that.'

'I'm not.' She picked the crust off a piece of bread and tried to make it into a circle. 'We're the same age, Sem.' She stopped playing with the bread and glared at him. 'So why do you always behave like my little brother?'

'I don't!' said Sem. 'I do *lots*. You've only got to ask. What have I done wrong now?'

'You make me cross,' said Cissy. 'That's all. I'm going to bed.'

Sem propped a book open against the teapot and ate his supper. When the meal was over he played patience for a while and hammered out a tune on the piano; then he saw that Cissy's food was still lying on the plate so he picked up a fork, mashed everything together and shaped it into a moat and battlements. Enthusiastic now, he looked in the workbox for a scrap of material to make a flag, tied it to a teaspoon and set it on a turret. The soldiers were peas, the invading army grains of rice from the cupboard.

By the time he'd finished the fire was nearly out and he couldn't be bothered to get more wood, so he left everything as it was and went upstairs to his room.

When Sem was a small boy he found a caterpillar on a lilac tree. He put it in a cup and asked his parents if he might keep it as a pet. 'You won't have it for long,' they told him. 'That's only a bit of its life, a first step.' His father built the caterpillar a wooden box, with a sheet of glass for a lid and fresh leaves for a carpet, telling Sem to be sure and add new leaves every day so that his pet would get fat. After a while the caterpillar disappeared and the whole family came to look. Cissy spotted it first: the dry brown chrysalis, mimicking a twig. 'Is it dead?' asked Sem.

'Just wait,' said his mother, taking the glass lid away. 'You'll get a surprise.'

The chrysalis split open one morning while Sem was having breakfast. When he saw what had happened, he ran to get Cissy and his parents and they all stood hand in hand around the box, looking at the newly born butterfly. Its wings were still tightly curled as it trembled on the dry leaves. 'What do we do now?' said Sem, wanting more.

'We give it time to find out who it is and then we let it fly away,' said his father, taking the box to the open window. And as the hours passed, with Cissy and Sem taking turns to keep watch, the butterfly stretched and flattened its wings and set off into the breeze, a dancing blue dot against the oranges and yellows of the garden. After that Sem always kept a caterpillar or a chrysalis in his room, never tiring of the moment when it grew up.

On the night that he'd made the castle out of Cissy's dinner, he went to bed without clearing away the plates or brushing his teeth. He wasn't tired enough to sleep so he picked up his book, quite unaware of the blue butterfly that was fluttering towards him. He'd found his place in the story and started to read when all at once the words convulsed, broke up and scattered on the page. Sem, immobilised and blinking, watched the letters as they scurried in a zig-zag over the paper. Then words started to shape themselves out of the confusion.

If you had a wish and a wish that might come true, what would you ask for ask for? said the writing, clear at last. Was the message meant for him? How was he to answer? He raised his head to think and saw the butterfly doing a little dance in the air above him. It flew down and walked delicately across the words, changing them as it went. *Answer me answer me.*

'Is it you I'm talking to?' said Sem, who'd been caught unawares twice now and was almost enjoying it.

Yes yes, said the butterfly and the book. *Will you wish and wish?*

'For anything?'

Anything and anything.

Sem thought of the many things he might wish for, some of them useful, some of them not. Then he remembered how unpleasant Cissy had been. 'I think I'll wish for Cissy to stop being so sensible,' he said, 'then she won't be cross with me.'

Is that your wish your wish?

'I do believe it is,' said Sem.

Then it's already true and it's true, said the book. The butterfly danced lightly over his hand and disappeared.

The next morning, when Sem came downstairs, Cissy was laughing at the castle he'd made out of her dinner. 'That's good,' she said, picking out the teaspoon and waving the flag so that bits of food fell on the carpet.

'Aren't you cross?' asked Sem.

'Why would I be cross?' said Cissy. 'Shall we go out soon? It's a lovely day.'

When they were in the village, a farmer came up to Cissy and asked her about a parcel he was expecting that hadn't arrived. 'I'm sure I don't know,' said Cissy, her fingers crossed behind her back. 'But everything's been delivered. Perhaps it'll come soon.' The farmer walked away, shaking his head. Cissy looked at Sem and put on a bad-tempered face. 'You did the delivery yesterday,' she said, in a voice just like the farmer. 'You're very, very naughty.' Then she grinned. 'Wasn't it in your sack?'

'Yes,' said Sem, sure now that the wish was working. 'But I got fed up. So I hid it under a bush. Actually, I hid a few.'

'What! That's awful!'

'We can go and get them if you like,' said Sem. 'Or we could leave them till tomorrow...'

'Might as well leave them,' said Cissy. 'Let's go for a walk.'

Sem's wish really had come true. Cissy didn't care about her work and she never got cross anymore. They played games and told stories and made up jokes and neither of them did any washing or mending or cleaning up. Before long there was no food left, except for the few things that had grown despite their lack of care; and when the day came that Sem's shirts had been in and out of the washing bag three times and his socks were so holey that they didn't cover any of his toes, he decided that he had to talk to Cissy. She was sitting on the floor, trying to master a trick with three cups and a marble.

'Do you think we should do a few chores?' he said.

'If you want.' Cissy lifted the cups. The marble had disappeared.

'There's nothing to eat,' said Sem. 'Except parsley.' Cissy didn't answer. She was trying to make the marble appear under each of the cups in turn. 'Don't worry about me then,' he said at the door.

'Don't worry, I won't.'

Sem went back to his room, realizing what a fool he'd been, wasting the good luck that had come his way. Without Cissy to organise them both, his life was miserable. He could have asked for a beautiful wife or eternal youth instead of wishing himself filthy shirts and an empty larder. He looked into the box where a new caterpillar was busy getting fat, then he lay on the bed and opened his book. If he read the same page, perhaps the butterfly would come back. Starting at the place where the writing had appeared all those weeks ago, he read the story again, turning the cover to make sure that the butterfly wasn't hiding anywhere. A sound had him running to the wardrobe but it was only an old hat slipping off a hook. Disappointed, he ruffled the curtains, looked under the bed and pulled back the dirty bedclothes but there was nothing more interesting than stale crumbs and a missing pencil. An idea struck him; he lifted the glass lid off the box and put the big green caterpillar gently on his book. It lay still for a moment, then heaved itself across the page, fell onto the table, wriggled twice and set off in search of food. Sem put it back on its leaves and then, thinking that he might as well sleep as be hungry, he puffed up the pillow and lay down.

A sensation, no heavier than breath, moved across his eyelids and down his cheek. He opened his eyes to see the blue butterfly poised on his knuckles. As he sat up, it fluttered to the mantlepiece and settled, trembling, while Sem went to the table and opened the book.

What a silly wish silly wish the words said. *Waste waste waste.*

'Why didn't you tell me?' asked Sem.

What now what now?

'I want everything to be back like it was before.' The butterfly didn't move; the book said nothing. 'That's not right is it?' said Sem. 'I didn't like how it was before.' He gazed at the page, trying to work out the consequences of his next request. 'Let's try both of us being sensible.'

Is that your wish your wish?

'Definitely,' said Sem, thinking about the terrible state of things.

Then it's already true and it's true said the book. The butterfly touched his face and disappeared.

He stared at the bedroom with new eyes. Dust lay everywhere and the sheets were as grey as squirrel fur. He picked up a great armful of dirty washing and set off down the stairs to find Cissy standing in the kitchen.

'Look at this!' she cried, showing him a lump of green mould at the bottom of the bread bin. 'And this!' The sink was full of dirty dishes sitting in slimy brown water. 'Why's everything so dirty?'

'Let's clean up,' said Sem. 'I'll get some wood to heat the water. You make a shopping list.'

'We can't go shopping?' said Cissy. 'We don't have a single penny!'

'I'll get work. Don't worry, Cissy. We'll think of a way.'

As soon as the schoolmaster knew that Sem was looking for a job, he asked him to help the children with their reading and writing.

Cleaves, who was ill again, went to stay with his sister and gave Cissy full charge of the post until he got back. Sem even found the parcels that he'd hidden and delivered them, apologizing for having dropped them on his round.

One evening, as Sem was correcting homework and Cissy was counting stamps, she leant back in her chair and sighed. 'I seem to remember,' she said, 'that we used to have fun.'

'We didn't have so much to do,' said Sem, knowing that the time had come to own up. 'Actually, I've got something to tell you.' He ran off to his room and came back with the book. 'I was reading,' he said, 'and then the words went all sparkly and a butterfly appeared and they wrote to me.'

'Who wrote to you?' asked Cissy.

'The words. In the book. And they asked if I had a wish.'

'And did you?'

'You were being cross all the time,' said Sem. 'I should have done my share of the work, but I asked if you could change instead.'

'Change how?'

'Not to be grown-up anymore.'

'Oh,' said Cissy. 'I see.'

He opened the book to show her where the words had been and pushed it across the table. 'There,' he said, pointing at the page. Cissy picked it up and peered at the lettering, running her finger along the lines. It was ordinary, a simple story.

'And then what happened?' she said. 'When you wished?'

'You stopped being sensible.'

'And everything started to go wrong –'

'Yes. But I got another chance. So I asked if we could both be grown-up. But now I know I should have asked for something in-between,' said Sem. 'Only I didn't have time to think. Not properly.'

'I wish I'd seen it,' she said, glancing down.

No more wishes no more wishes said the book. 'Don't move,' whispered Sem. 'The butterfly, it's on your hair.'

'Oh!' said Cissy, her face as bright as a child's. 'Please ask now. Ask if we can change.'

'I know you've said no more wishes,' said Sem, addressing the butterfly, 'but if I'm not mistaken, three's the rule. So do you think that we could be a bit grown-up and a bit not?'

I only do two do two said the book. *So it's up to you to you to you. Goodbye and goodbye. Goodbye...*

As the writing faded, the butterfly fluttered down to Cissy's hand and then flew to Sem, touching his face softly before vanishing somewhere near the ceiling. Cissy drank the last of her tea and turned the cup upside down on the table. 'Look under there,' she said.

Sem lifted the cup. There were two big, blue shiny marbles.

'Bet you couldn't do that,' said Cissy.

'Bet I could,' said Sem.

Cancer

Thomas Coates

homas Coates skimmed the pale yellow cream from the milk pans and ladled it into the churn. He never tired of his mornings, listening for the first slip-slops of the cream as it thickened into butter, then the patting of it and the wrapping of it and the stacking of it in the big wicker baskets. When they were all lined up, neat as neat along the wall, he filled a bowl with skimmed milk and took it to his little dog, Elsie, who was waiting patiently outside the door.

And there was his aunt, on time as always, bustling up the path and calling to him as she neared the dairy. 'Are you ready, Thomas?'

'*We're* ready,' called his uncle, bustling up behind. 'And you want to mind that dog,' he added, as if he hadn't said the same thing to Thomas every morning for years and years. 'We don't want her running under the cart, do we?'

'No, uncle,' said Thomas, loading up the butter. 'I'll be sure and mind the dog.'

When they'd gone off to market, he walked through the gardens to the house with Elsie at his heels. His mother was waiting for him, sitting at the far end of the table in her big chair. 'I've just heard about a competition for best cheese,' she said, looking at him over her spectacles. 'What do you think of that?'

'I know about it, if that's what you mean and we could win, if that's what you're asking.'

'Will you be going then?' Her face was impassive but Thomas sensed that he was being asked a testing question.

'Do you want me to?' he said.

'You'd be away for a long time, two weeks or more.'

'Ah,' said Thomas, understanding. 'I don't think I'll bother then.' The matter decided, he made a pot of tea and buttered them each a scone.

Every evening, after a long cosy supper, the family went early to bed. Except for Thomas that is, whose habit was to take Elsie for a walk, lock up and then sit by the last embers of the fire until he was tired enough to sleep. But this night, this magical night, the air was sweet with honeysuckle and a bright full moon shone silver on the grass. Thomas didn't want to waste the beauty of it, so they went a little further than they might have done, Elsie leading them both to the narrow river that marked the edge of their private land.

A wood, once belonging to the family, stretched ahead of them for miles beyond the water. His great-grandparents had built a bridge to make it possible to walk there and take picnics, but the new owner had left the place to look after itself so that now the bridge was crumbling and the trees were dense and dark. Thomas found them forbidding and preferred to look away, at the sky or at the flowers by the water's edge. He threw Elsie a stick to lure her back.

'Here!' he shouted, 'Now!'

But he might as well have been talking to himself. With a little yelp of excitement, she ran over the bridge and disappeared. Clinging to the parapet, Thomas walked warily to the centre; the lapping of the stream below his feet was loud in the silence. He didn't like it there but even so, out of care for Elsie, he whistled and waited for a good long time before deciding that she could be summoned just as well from the bank. Just as he was lifting his foot to walk away, she trotted out of the trees.

Behind her, wearing a dress like knitted milk, was a young woman with long white-gold hair. She stepped onto the bridge and came to the centre with Elsie at her side.

Thomas didn't know what to say so he spoke to Elsie instead. 'Where have you been?' he said. 'Worrying me like that!'

'She came to find me,' said the woman. 'I called her.'

'Did you?'

'My name's Lily,' she said, bending down to stroke the dog. 'And you're Thomas.'

'How do you know that?' said Thomas. 'How do you know me?'

'I've been waiting.'

'For *me?*' Thomas pointed behind her, to the trees. 'Is that where you live?'

'Not really. I pass through it.'

'From where?'

But she didn't reply. And for what seemed to Thomas like hours and hours, they stood, face to face, not quite looking at each other but not quite looking away.

A bird began to sing. 'I'm going now,' she whispered. 'Will you come back tomorrow?'

'When?' said Thomas.

'Late. With the moon.'

He watched her walk into the wood. The birds were all singing now and the first pale stripes of dawn were lighting up the sky.

'Come on, Elsie,' he said. 'Let's go home.'

The porridge was delicious. Thomas cut his spoon into the edge, where it was cool, so that the cream could run in and fill the gap.

'*Thomas Coates!*' His mother was laughing. 'That's the third time your father's asked you about the dairy roof.' She passed his chair and put her fingers round the back of his neck. 'You'll be telling me you're in love next!' Thomas looked up and saw the faces staring at him round the table.

'Sorry?' he said. 'Have I missed something?' Everybody laughed. For a moment, Thomas thought that he might explain about Lily, but he couldn't find a way to begin and then he couldn't see the point, so in the end he had another bowl of porridge and reassured his father that he'd look at the roof without fail.

The day passed very slowly. During dinner his grandmother started to talk about her childhood, and then they all told stories about people in the family who were no longer there and stories about people who were. Thomas wanted to change into his best shirt and run to Lily but every time he went to stack the plates somebody would say, 'Leave those, we haven't finished...' or 'For goodness' sake, sit down and listen...' until he was so peeved that he could have whisked off the tablecloth and flung the dishes to the floor.

When all the goodnights had finally been said, Thomas opened the front door and looked out. The sky was clear. 'I'll take Elsie for her walk,' he said.

'Can't you just let her out of the back door?' said his mother. 'It's very late.' She patted his cheek and kissed him. 'If you must go, do put on your jacket. You'll catch cold in that thin shirt.'

Lily was waiting on the bridge and Elsie ran straight to her outstretched hand, barking with excitement. Thomas watched them, his eyes brimming with tears. 'I'm sorry I'm late,' he said.

'I knew you'd come,' she whispered, reaching him and standing close. 'Tell me what you've been feeling today.'

'Things about you, mostly,' said Thomas, hardly believing that he could be so honest. 'You certainly did fill my mind.' Suddenly, they were holding hands; her skin was cool. She led him to the parapet. Below them in the river the moon lay full. A frog rustled through the reeds and splashed into the water.

'Tell me how you know me,' said Thomas, his voice too loud in his own ears.

'I've been watching,' said Lily, 'and I thought I'd be your sweetheart, so I called Elsie and she brought you here.'

'I've never had a sweetheart,' said Thomas. 'Never felt the need.' In a flash, he imagined bringing a stranger into the house. 'There's a lot of us,' he explained, 'and we all have our little ways...'

Lily kissed his cheek, then he put his arm round her and she rested her head against his shoulder.

Too soon, the first bird called up the dawn and Thomas knew that he would have to get home to bed before his mother came to wake him. Lily held him close. 'I'll be waiting,' she said, 'dear, sweet Thomas.' After saying goodbye to Elsie, she walked off the bridge and into the wood, looking back often to blow kisses, until she'd disappeared behind the trees.

Exhausted, Thomas slept deeply for half an hour before his mother knocked at the door. 'Milk's arrived!' she called. He stumbled out of bed, half asleep, and dressed himself in the clothes he'd left lying on the floor. When the milk was safely in the pans, he went back to wash and change. His mother was waiting by the stairs.

'You look dreadful,' she said, holding him by the arm and staring into his face.

'I haven't been sleeping very well, that's all.' Thomas smiled at her. 'You start breakfast, I'll be down in a minute.' Not sure whether to believe him, she held on for a moment longer, then shrugged and smiled back.

'You're a good boy,' she said, patting his cheek.

After breakfast Thomas made the butter, badly, forgetting to do this and forgetting to do that. By the time he'd got everything right and lined up the baskets, he knew that he'd have to tell his mother about the meeting on the bridge.

They sat together at the kitchen table, shelling peas. As he did his best to describe Lily, Thomas was surprised by how little he knew. In fact, as his mother remarked, he only knew what was in front of his nose, not a thing more. 'You haven't even asked her where she's from,' said his mother, in amazement. She rubbed her fingernail along the soft smooth peapod. 'What on earth did you find to talk about?'

Thomas looked helplessly at the colander. 'I don't know.'

'Oh, Thomas!' His mother threw the pod onto the table and folded her arms. 'I think it's time you two had a proper talk. Who her family is, where they live, what they're doing letting her wander about in the middle of the night. That sort of thing.' She picked up the colander and stopped by his chair to give him a hug. 'Be careful. I don't want you hurt.'

He couldn't see Lily at first; she was in the shadows, near the wood. As Elsie ran up, she lifted her close and pressed her face into the little dog's neck.

Thomas was so full of his mother's questions that he couldn't think of anything ordinary to say to her. 'I can't see you very well,' he said. 'The moon isn't so bright.'

'It's waning now,' said Lily. 'Soon it'll whittle away to nothing.' She put Elsie down and stood still, waiting for Thomas to speak.

'There are some things I need to ask you,' he said. He looked so miserable that Elsie began to whimper.

'What sort of things?'

'Where you're from,' he said. 'And how you know me.'

'I know you're kind and good,' said Lily. 'Isn't that enough?' She reached out and Thomas gripped her hand like a man falling off a cliff.

'And where you live,' he pleaded, pointing at the wood. 'You can't live in there!'

'If you came with me,' said Lily. 'I'd look after you always.'

'But I promised I'd find out,' said Thomas, imagining his mother there, shaking her head as she looked at them both. 'Why don't you come home with me?'

'I can't!' said Lily.

'*Why not?*' cried Thomas. 'Why is this all so difficult?'

'I've made a promise too,' said Lily. 'And I can't cross this bridge, not ever.' Lily looked away, up at the sky. 'I might as well go back,' she said. 'I can't bear this.' She knelt down and whispered to Elsie, then turned without saying goodbye and walked away into the trees.

Elsie came to Thomas and sat sadly at his feet. 'I'm sorry girl,' he said, through his tears. 'Let's go home.'

He told the family over breakfast. 'I had a bad feeling about the whole thing,' his mother said, looking round the table for support. 'So you never found out who she was?'

'I don't think she wanted me to know,' said Thomas, spreading too much butter on his toast and eating it anyway.

'You must be tired,' said his grandmother, 'staying up until all hours.'

'I think that girl's nothing but a nuisance,' said his father, reaching over to pat Thomas on the hand. 'I'm of a mind to meet her. What do you say we all go tonight? Show her what she's up against. Stand up for our boy.'

'I'm not sure she'd like that,' said Thomas.

'I'm for it,' said his aunt.

'That's settled then,' said his mother, and everyone nodded. 'We'll go after dinner.'

Thomas and Elsie led the way. 'I don't like it here,' said his uncle, holding the lantern high. 'It must be years since I walked through this field.'

'I never liked it,' said his grandmother. 'I hope she's worth it, this girl.'

The sky was cloudy, the moon shrinking. By the time they got to the river it was too dark to see what lay on the other side. 'Is this what usually happens?' said his father. 'How do you let her know you're here?'

'Elsie gets her,' said Thomas. They watched as the dog ran to the middle of the bridge. 'Fetch Lily,' said Thomas, but Elsie lay down with her head on her paws and her ears flat against her head.

Thomas looked at his family, a strange little army gathered in the dark. 'She won't go in,' he said. 'And Lily's nowhere to be seen.'

An owl screeched behind him. He looked back into the trees. Was that her? That white curve, high up in the branches? Leaving Elsie, he walked towards the wood, his nails digging into the palms of his hands.

'You're not to go in there!' cried his mother. He stopped. The trees towered over him, the darkness was absolute. The owl screeched again and all at once, Thomas feared for his life. He turned and ran, scooping Elsie into his arms and not stopping until the bridge was a very long way behind.

Later, they sat in the kitchen and drank tea by the fire.

'You're better off,' said his father. 'A girl like that.'

'You want a nice girl you can bring home,' said his grandmother, topping up the teapot. 'Someone more convenient.'

'There's a bit of a dance at the village hall tomorrow,' said his uncle. 'You could find a new sweetheart quick as a wink. Why don't you go?'

'We'll all go,' said his mother. 'It's high time you had a sweetheart of your own.'

'I'm not sure I want to go anywhere,' said Thomas. 'Me and Elsie, we'll be alright for a bit.'

His mother cut slices from a slab of fruit bread. 'We'll take you to the dance,' she said firmly, 'and that's the end of it. Now drink your tea.'

'Suppose I wanted to go by myself?' said Thomas. There was a long pause.

'Well, if you don't want us to come...' said his mother, putting down the knife.

Thomas didn't say anything. He was remembering Lily blowing kisses at him from her side of the bridge. He got up and walked to the window.

'You come back here, Thomas Coates. Your tea's poured!'

'In a minute,' he said, opening the curtains and looking out. 'There'll be a new moon tomorrow night. I might just go down to the river and see if she's there.'

Leo
The King

he King draped himself over a tapestry chair and dipped a pastry into a glass of sweet white wine. 'Tell me,' he said, addressing the Fool. 'What are you trying to do?'

'Well,' said the Fool, who was juggling fried sardines with slices of bread and a plate. 'I intend to toss this lot in the air and astonish you with a perfect pile of sandwiches, crusts off.'

'Hurrah,' said the King. 'Awfully good.'

'Too noisy,' said the cat, Koshka.

The Fool assembled the sandwiches, ate them, threw the sardine tails onto the cat's plate and wiped his fingers clean with a lavender scented handkerchief. Sardine and lavender was oddly worse than sardine by itself. 'Now,' he said, putting his hands deep into his trouser pockets, 'I shall recite a ballad.'

But no sooner had he cleared his throat than a large servant, grotesque in satin, burst through the door. 'I've looked high and low,' he said, severely, bowing to the King. 'You shouldn't have hidden, sire, not today.'

'Don't be tiresome, Wigg.' The King sat up. 'Can't bear watching all that *fuss*.'

Wigg was adamant: it was time to show themselves. So with Koshka bringing up the rear, they all trooped downstairs. Great branches of sweet-smelling orange blossom tumbled from baskets on the floor and hung from every corner of the banqueting hall; a canopy of yellow silk caught up with garlands of marigolds and lemons made a bower over the table; the cloth, as long as a field, was embroidered with stars and laid with golden plates and pyramids of candied fruit.

'Marvellous!' said the King, taking a sugar-plum and eating it whole.

The guests at the King's Revel were chosen by lot from every village and hamlet to attend with gifts and be feasted in return. His people, for the most part, were quite poor and had little interest in dressing up or giving anything precious away. But with neighbourly goodwill they helped each other out, borrowing shoes from here and a hat from there; weeding or cooking or cleaning in exchange for a gift to take to the palace.

As the King was eating the plum, a subdued queue was beginning to form at the palace gates. The clock struck twelve. 'I'm going to dress,' he said. 'You can let them in when I'm ready.'

The Fool stood behind the King's chair and watched the feast while Koshka circled the room, demanding attention. When the last scraps of food had been eaten, or slipped into pockets and purses, Wigg took a small hammer from his belt and struck a gong: a signal to the guests that it was time to line up with their presents. The queue took so long to establish that by the time everyone had found a place, the King was sound asleep. Prodded gently by the Fool, he looked up to find a farmer presenting him with a large basket, covered with a lumpy cloth.

'And what have you got in there?' said the King, trying to keep his eyes open.

'It's a young boar, your Majesty,' said the farmer. 'Should grow well for you, given care.' Lowering his head, he walked away backwards and handed the basket to a footman. There was a sudden commotion as the little boar escaped from its basket and shot off into the crowd. All attention was given to the chase and the King found himself sitting alone, watching the room. The squealing pig and its pursuers led his eye from place to place and at first he saw what he expected to see: his people, merry with giving and a fine meal.

But then, as if he had stumbled over a stone and revealed some horror beneath, he overheard a servant whispering *'Cheer up or else'* to a woman as he pinched her cruelly on the arm. Behind her, a man hit out at his grim wife and fretful children... so many sullen faces...

'They hate me!' cried the King.

'As kind as knives,' said the Fool. 'Cut through cheese in no time.'

The boar was caught and the queue reformed but for the King, the day had lost all its sweetness. Koshka woke from his sleep, certain of a drama, and jumped onto the throne. 'What's up?' he said. 'What have I missed?'

The Fool sat quietly, humming to himself.

When the day was over, the King went wretchedly to bed and lay awake until the Fool and Koshka brought in his morning tea. They found him in his nightshirt staring sightlessly at a hand mirror.

'No sleep?' enquired the Fool.

The King dropped the mirror and looked about him, finally resting his gaze on the face of his dearest friend. 'You too?' he said. 'Do they pinch *you* and threaten worse?'

'Not that I've noticed,' said the Fool, 'but then I'm hardly worth the effort.'

'I've got pins and needles in my heart,' said the King, clutching at his chest. 'How do I make them love me, Fool? Am I such a rotten King?'

The Fool's face went blank, a sure sign that he was deep in thought and likely to come up with a pithy piece of common sense disguised as folklore. 'I've heard it said, sire, that only a humble man...'

'Humble!' shouted the King, bounding out of bed.

'Humble in his inmost...' The Fool tried to finish the sentence but the King was dancing on the spot, deaf to interruption.

'That's *it*! I shall share their poverty! Live in squalor! Grow peacocks! Cook! Make my own bed and... and... *dress myself*! How they'll love me!'

The Fool was struck dumb. The theme of his text had been scuppered and chaos was inevitable. Before he could think of any useful intervention the King had already left the bedchamber, clapping his hands and calling joyfully for servants to start the great work of impoverishing the royal household.

Koshka stared at himself in the mirror, now lying forgotten on the carpet. 'What about me?' he said. 'Don't I get a word in?'

The ministers gathered in the throne room to protest. 'Isn't this exciting?' cried the King, sitting on the floor and waving at them all to follow suit. 'Might as well start as we mean to go on, don't you think? No need for fuss and bother now. I'm ordinary, just like you.' The ministers began to shout in protest but the King silenced them. 'I am not loved,' he said, with dignity. Nobody spoke. The King persevered. 'My intention is this. I shall have a small shack built for me in the palace grounds and I shall live there with the Fool and the cat, Koshka. And a bucket. For the well.'

The Fool, sitting close by the King, looked round at the open mouths of the ministers and smiled, loyally.

'I have seen servants,' said the King, 'with sharp noses and cruel faces. They have no place in my court. You may all stay here if you wish, but you must live simply. The people must see that we are humble and worthy of their love.'

With a flourish, the King leapt up and walked rapturously to the door with his head high and the Fool cartwheeling behind. There was a pause and then uproar as the ministers struggled to their feet, shouting and waving papers. The Fool turned at the door and waved his hat so that the bells on it rang out clearly through the hubbub. 'The sun shines equally on us all,' he said quietly. 'Trite but true.'

The next few days were busy. Wood for the shack had to be weathered in a rush so that it might look suitably shabby. The King was to have one small room to himself, the Fool another and they would share a third for meals. They would sleep on narrow planks of wood with thin straw mattresses, rough grey blankets and one small hard pillow each, covered in striped ticking. Water would be drawn each day from the well and a tin basin set aside for washing.

As the King had never taken the slightest notice of his gardens and hardly knew the difference between a tree and a spade, the gardeners were to clear the undergrowth around the shack and prepare the ground for sowing. The King would then plant seedlings and tend them, eating whatever he could grow. Under his big four-poster, now bare of drapes and with several fewer pillows, he was filling a box with special things: a mirror, scissors and a comb, a penny-whistle, a toothpick, a jar of boiled sweets and two handkerchiefs in case he caught a cold.

Koshka was unhappy. 'I'm not staying in that hovel!' he complained. 'Grey blankets! Who do you think I am?' But the King was resolute and Koshka took to visiting the building site with little parcels of food that he hid in the undergrowth and marked with his scent.

The Fool was unusually gloomy. Although he was never without a useful analogy, ballad or paradox, the awful speed with which his life had run amok had left him repeating the old and trusted, his wits slack.

On moving day, the cat remained rebelliously silent but the King and the Fool rather enjoyed themselves, delighting in the shack in much the same way that they might have delighted in going to the circus. The beds were unyielding and the food dreary, but it was pleasantly tiring to do a little gardening and to light a fire with the wood that they'd gathered themselves from the heap the gardeners had left by the side wall.

'Well, I say! I certainly earned my supper!' said the King on the first night, as he tried to lounge on a wooden chair with one foot on the corner of the stove and the other on the table. 'Tell me a story, Fool. Something agricultural...' But the King was asleep before the Fool could think of anything interesting to say, so he washed the dishes instead and went to bed on his thin straw mattress.

They soon slipped into a routine. Koshka found that he could get to the palace, take something delicious from the kitchen table, have a nap on a bed somewhere and be back before he was missed. None of the vegetables did terribly well as neither of them remembered to water the garden, but they scraped enough food together to eat one good meal a day.

Every morning the King would lean over the low fence around the little shack and watch people as they passed by, calling 'Good morning to you!' or 'What lovely weather this is!' but he never got more than a mumble in response. 'I don't know what I'm supposed to say to him,' said a woman to her husband as they hurried away. 'Do you think he's addled?'

The children laughed at him behind his back and pretended to be Kings and Queens in crowns made of string and dead flowers. On market day, nobody would take his money and if he tried to barter eggs for candles or salt, the traders dealt with the Fool and left the King standing there alone, the empty basket dangling foolishly from his hand.

In a few short weeks, he began to feel that he was invisible to everyone but the Fool and the cat. 'The whole *point* of this awful life is to make the people love me and they don't and I'm thoroughly bored with it, so there,' he said, poking the fire and glaring at the Fool. 'You *promised* that being humble would do the trick and here I am in rags and tatters and no one even says good morning!'

The Fool spluttered into his tea. 'What do you mean I *promised?*'

'You know you did! Why else would I have left my lovely palace and moved into this awful hole with you?' The King put his head into his hands and sobbed. It was only self-pity, but a touching sight nonetheless, and the Fool was moved.

'Now look here,' he soothed. 'When I said that only a humble man –'

'It was rubbish!' said the King, his face pink and soggy.

'*When* I said that,' said the Fool, firmly, 'I was trying to tell you that a truly humble man needs to be humble in his heart, not in his habits.'

'I don't understand, I never understand,' moaned the King. 'Why do you always say such clever things and then I don't know what you mean even when I think about them afterwards?'

The Fool wasn't absolutely sure what he meant himself. 'I think I can safely say,' he ventured, 'that a humble man, being wise, has the sense to put his heart in the right place.'

'What? *What?* What do you mean the right place?' cried the King, more anxious than ever to be wise, humble and happy all at once.

'Oh, I don't know!' shouted the Fool, standing on his head. 'Give me a chance to work it out!' An hour passed, while the King tried to doze and the Fool ruminated. 'I've got it,' he said at last. 'Listen...'

And they sat up all night, talking close to the stove, until the wood ran out and they had to fetch their blankets. The cold morning air made them hungry so they breakfasted on the last of some flat bread and cold carrots. Then the Fool went to the palace, told Wigg to bring suitable clothing to the shack and arranged for the King to be collected in the state coach at noon.

The King, the Fool and Koshka went home. 'About time too,' said Koshka. 'Backwards and forwards. I was worn out.' Nobody was particularly pleased to see them but as the palace was more or less unchanged, despite the King's previous orders to the contrary, it took no time at all for everything to get back to normal.

'I've been terribly ordinary,' he explained to the chancellor, 'and it didn't help a bit. Now I shall act like a King, but be humble in my inmost heart.'

'And how will you do that, your Majesty?' said the chancellor, longing to have the palace to himself again.

'You'll see, dear boy,' said the King. 'You'll see!'

The Fool somersaulted a few times and landed on his hands. 'It's a poor servant that has no master,' he said. 'Banal but blunt.'

'And show a bit of respect in future,' said Koshka, pulling a loose thread in the chancellor's robe and undoing the hem.

'I think we'll have a party!' said the King. 'And we'll ask *everybody* to come. We'll have dancing and singing and games and absolutely no pinching and prodding. And I don't want any presents. Is that understood?'

And of course it was the best party there ever was, in the palace or out of it. 'I'm so pleased to see you all here!' he said, over and over again, as he shook hands with every man, woman and child in the ballroom. And after supper, they danced all night while the world turned away from the sun and came back again for morning. Breakfast was laid in the garden for anyone who wanted it and every child was given a gingerbread man in a little tin box as a keepsake.

At the end of the party, the King stood at the palace doors and said goodbye to everyone, while the Fool stole pennies from their ears and Koshka prowled between them and was made a fuss of.

As the last family walked away, the King turned to the Fool. 'I've just thought of an idea for a play!' he said.

'Fancy that!' said the Fool. 'I was cooking up a poem about a firefly and a carpetbag.'

'We'll do yours first,' said the King, hugging a small child who'd run back to thank him for the gingerbread. 'And then we'll do mine. It's going to be a comedy.'

'Of course it is,' said the Fool. 'What else?'

Virgo
Kate

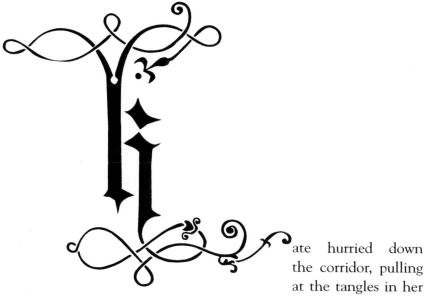ate hurried down the corridor, pulling at the tangles in her hair. The door to the meeting room was closed! She knocked, got no answer, steadied herself and knocked again.

'I heard you!' Knowle, her tutor, opened the door. He was scowling. 'You're seventeen minutes late. Junior reports have finished.'

'I'm sorry,' she said. 'I overslept.'

'That's a poor excuse. I'll see what I can do. Don't make a noise.'

Kate crept past him and stood by the wall, listening to the seniors as they discussed a case.

'...and that awful Neville Knox just won't stop,' the woman at the head of the table was saying. 'If his neighbour's cat so much as puts a paw in his garden, Neville piles all his rubbish on her front lawn.' She looked down at her notes. 'We sent another junior last week.'

'Visible?' asked the man beside her.

'No, invisible. They've all run out of ideas. I think I'll have to go myself. I went last year, when he was taking their washing off the line and boiling it. He said he couldn't bear the stains.'

One of the seniors noticed Kate. 'You shouldn't be in here now,' he said.

'Indeed she shouldn't.' Knowle took Kate's arm and they stepped forward. 'Please tell the table why you were late.'

'I overslept. I'm very sorry.'

'And if you'd been here on time, would you have had anything to report?'

'Oh, yes.' She picked up her notes and rummaged through them. 'I've got... oh dear... I'm so sorry, really, so sorry... I've got the wrong...'

'We're here to help people,' sighed Knowle. 'I don't know how you can expect to do that when you can barely help yourself.'

Everyone at the table was observing her, their kind, serious faces inviting her to speak. She swallowed hard and did her best to stand straight. 'I'll see what I can do without notes,' she said.

'Go on then.' Knowle, rested his chin in his cupped hands. 'We're listening.'

'I was told I could choose from the level two board,' said Kate, 'and they're all quite difficult cases.' She looked along the row of seniors, anxious that she should be making a good impression after her awkward start. A few of them smiled.

'Yes,' said Knowle. 'Difficult.'

'I've chosen someone called the Reader.' There was a murmur of interest. 'Her job is to inspect the Lists and Chronicles looking for spelling mistakes and proper punctuation. If she finds anything that makes no sense, she has to change it altogether. It's very hard work. And she never does anything else. Not even on feast days,' she added, remembering a footnote on page two of the absent file.

The seniors nodded. 'The Reader appealed to us all,' said one. 'And what do you think she needs?'

'I haven't quite decided,' said Kate.

'Indeed,' said Knowle.

'But I think I could start by giving her something different to look at. You know, a change of perspective.' The seniors nodded again, more vigorously.

'And how do you intend to do that?' asked Knowle.

'With a window,' said Kate. 'And that's all I know at present.'

The report was over. The seniors began to speak amongst themselves. Knowle pointed at the instruction manual in Kate's hand.

'We didn't write this to press flowers in. Do read it occasionally. And if you can't wake up on time, then get a new clock. Good work can't be done in a muddle. Or in a hurry...'

The Reader sat hunched at her desk, pen in hand, lit by a row of lamps on a shelf behind her head. Her face was almost obscured by a large pair of curious spectacles, opaque but for a small hole in each blacked-out lens. This tiny hole had been fitted with a special magnifying glass to concentrate her view, so that the smallest error stood out and signalled itself to be corrected.

The Reader, with or without her spectacles, would not have seen Kate, who was now invisible and standing by the door, scrutinizing the gloomy room for useful information. Every inch of the sagging shelves that lined the walls was filled with ledgers and files. There were no paintings or flowers or ornaments. What little wall she could see was covered with yellowing paper, embossed with punctuation marks. There was no window.

Now what? Kate couldn't go back to the seniors without a plan.

The Reader took off her spectacles and cupped her hands over her red-rimmed eyes. This was a perfect moment, Kate decided, to make a suggestion. She knelt by the desk and looked at the Reader. 'If you had something else to look at,' she said loudly, 'something unfamiliar, your eyes wouldn't get so sore.'

The Reader rubbed her neck. Kate tried again.

'You're shrinking into your work...' she said, more loudly this time. 'You're as small as a semi-colon. You're as condensed as a comma...'

The Reader hunched her shoulders and dropped a little closer to the page.

'You're a full stop!' shouted Kate.

The Reader's nose was almost on the paper.

'How ridiculous it is,' said Kate, whispering in her ear, 'that your world should be reduced to a dot of ink. Why not look at something restful every now and then? A window for instance, wouldn't that be nice?'

The Reader stood up and looked about her, as if in search of an intruder. 'How strange,' she said. 'I could have sworn I heard a voice.'

The following morning, Kate found the Reader talking to a woman she assumed must be the office warden. 'I'm in great need of something restful to look at,' the Reader was saying. 'Do you have any ideas?'

'I don't know if I do,' said the warden. 'Perhaps you could look out of the window?'

'I don't *have* a window,' said the Reader. 'Obviously.'

The warden looked round the room. 'You're absolutely right. I suppose we'd better get you one.'

The Reader put her spectacles back on. 'I'd be grateful. And do please see that there's no mess.'

Kate went straight to Knowle. 'I think it's going quite well,' she said. 'The Reader's getting a window.'

'And what will you do when she has it? Trust to luck?'

'I'll see what she does next, I suppose,' said Kate, who was piqued to be put on the spot again.

Knowle handed her the manual. 'Read me the marked passage, if you will.'

Kate knew the words by heart. 'Banish woolly thinking!' she declaimed, without looking at the page. 'Never guess when you can know. Observation is the greatest tool in your possession; you must familiarize yourself with every aspect of your task before you blunder in. Beware impulse. Revere discretion.'

'That's right, Kate dear,' said Knowle, taking the book from her. 'So just stay alert, do your best and you'll avoid surprises.'

Even though the workmen were under strict orders not to talk, there was still a great deal of noise and mess as they hammered out bricks and put in the wooden window frame. Sheets had been draped over the bookshelves and spread on the bare portion of her desk but the Reader, having resisted all requests to move out of the room, was constantly having to wipe her spectacles and shake out the scarf that protected her mouth and nose.

As the day went on and the dust thickened and gathered on the pages, she began to correct smuts and specks, believing them to be misplaced punctuation. After rubbing at yet another grimy mark and tearing a hole in a document, she confronted the foreman. 'I'm sorry,' she said. 'But you'll have to stop. I'm at the end of my tether.' Kate leaped out of her chair, but the foreman was speaking before she could step in.

'You can't expect us to leave things like this!' he said, outraged. 'You asked for a window, not a hole in the wall.'

'Its taking too long,' said the Reader. 'Can't you just fill the hole up?'

'We've been here for two days,' said the foreman, gritting his teeth. 'We'll be finished in two more. That's not a long time for a quality bit of work, if I might say so.'

'Only two days,' said Kate to the Reader. 'It'll pass in no time. You could work in another room and you do so want a window.'

The Reader looked from left to right and from ceiling to floor, believing Kate's voice to be her own reasonable self. 'You're absolutely right,' she said to the foreman. 'I shall go to another room. Please continue.'

In two days, as promised, the builders had gone. Another whole day passed while the warden cleaned up the mess, then the Reader put on her correcting spectacles and checked the shelves for dust. The warden had been thorough; the room was spotless.

'Thank goodness,' said the Reader. 'What a horrible week.' As she spoke, she walked to the window and opened it, intending to assess the quality of the frame, but a gust of wind exploded into the room, whipping all the papers up into the air and dropping them higgledy-piggledy on the floor. Screaming for the warden, she slammed the window shut.

Kate, who'd just arrived, screamed with her and watched helplessly as the Reader scrabbled about on the floor, picking up her work. The warden came in without knocking. 'Are you alright?' she said. 'Only I thought I heard a cry.'

'Do please arrange for large, thick curtains to be put across that window,' said the Reader. 'There are vexing draughts.'

By the next morning, Kate had composed herself. She faced the seniors with her notes in order and gave her account of the previous day's crisis, admitting her lack of foresight. Knowle lifted his hand to stop her. 'Well, what now?' he said.

'I think I know what to do –'

'Good,' said Knowle, interrupting her. 'You may sit down. Who's next?'

Kate stood by the Reader's desk and stared at the back of her neck. The room was stuffier than ever. 'What you're missing,' said Kate, 'is blue sky and warm earth, daylight, fluffy clouds, a nice lawn...'

The Reader put down her pen, walked over to the heavy velvet curtains and pulled them open. As they parted and daylight fell on her face, she stood gazing out without expression. Then, with a little snort of disappointment, she turned away. Kate strode over to the window: a barren landscape stretched far into the distance. There were no trees or flowers, only stones and dry soil. This world was desolate and ugly. There was no view. Knowle would be very cross with her for not thinking ahead.

Before Kate could decide what to do next, the Reader opened the door and called for the warden. She came quickly, mop in hand. Kate could hardly breathe, she was so anxious. What would she do if the Reader asked for the window to be bricked up again?

'I don't want to be a nuisance,' said the Reader to the warden, 'but the world outside is rather dismal. Do you think that you could possibly arrange something nice for me to look at?'

Kate had a good supper and slept as if she'd been running up mountains. In the morning she went to see how the view was coming along.

'It should take about a week, ma'am,' the warden was saying. 'I do hope to see you content at last.' She backed out of the room and closed the door. The Reader mumbled her thanks and drew the curtains more closely together to block out the noise.

On the morning of the unveiling, Kate was called to Knowle's office. 'So the Reader will see her garden,' he said. 'And all will be well.'

'I hope so,' said Kate, worry starting up like a whisk. 'Have I made a mistake?'

'Observation,' sighed Knowle.

The Reader's room was as gloomy as ever. The lamps at her back illuminated her work; the rest was shadow.

'Excuse me, ma'am.' The warden was at the door. 'They're ready for you.'

'I must finish these amendments,' said the Reader, 'Be kind enough to come back later.'

'I'm sorry ma'am, but the gardeners are all waiting.'

Kate stood at the Reader's side, tapping her foot with exasperation. 'Please get up,' she said. 'You have to see what they've done. You can't wait any longer. You're curious. You're intrigued. You want to be nice to the warden, you're grateful to her. You really do want to look *now*.'

The Reader blotted the work and put her pen carefully on its stand. 'You're right,' she said to the warden as she walked to the window. 'I mustn't keep the gardeners from their work.'

She parted the curtains and leant forward to inspect the view. But what was this? A yellow blade of grass, a weed straggling onto the path, a worm slinking into a flower bud, a bough of lilac, breaking...

'I don't like this view at all,' said the Reader. 'I'm so terribly sorry. I think perhaps I've wasted everybody's time.'

The warden came to the window. 'Please ma'am, if you would.' She reached up gently and took off the Reader's correcting spectacles. 'Look again, ma'am. Please.'

And now the Reader saw the view. She saw paths prettily lined with plants, an arbour to read in, a waving bank of ferns and, right beside her window, a little quince tree, bright with blossom.

'Why!' she said, clapping her hands. 'It's beautiful!' The gardeners applauded, the warden smiled and Kate sat on the floor and wondered what on earth she was going to say to Knowle.

'So she looked at it without her spectacles?' Knowle said. 'And you persuaded her to do that, did you?'

'Not exactly.'

'*What* exactly?'

'The warden did it. In the end.'

'And who was the warden?'

'I don't know. Just a warden, I suppose.'

'Never guess when you can know. Have you got your manual? Look at the back, at the list of seniors on permanent, visible placement. You'll find someone called Naomi. Page two hundred and seven, line six.'

Kate ran her finger down the list. There she was. Naomi: Senior – Grade two.

'Do I know her?' said Kate.

'Naomi,' said Knowle, 'is your warden.'

'She isn't!'

'She is!' said Knowle. 'And she says that, with a lot of hard work, you're going to be quite good...'

Libra

Mr Spoons

r Spoons, the matchmaker, caught sight of his face in the mirror and smoothed the hair away from his eyes. 'Not bad for your age, Spoons,' he said. 'Not bad at all!' His mornings, as he liked to advise his patrons, were his busy times. He spent them in close study of his filing system: a selection of biscuit tins, blue for men and pink for women, three of each to cover the alphabet and all richly decorated by Mr Spoons himself.

He picked up a new request and studied it carefully. A rich and cantankerous elderly farmer was looking for a useful wife. Reaching for the first pink tin, he pulled out a dog-eared card from the back. 'Mrs Duddle,' he read aloud. "Widowed, children grown, good with livestock, presently indifferent to romance." Perfect!' said Mr Spoons, and joined them together with a pin.

In the afternoons, Mr Spoons and his neighbour, Peacey, took tea in the summer-house. After the first cup, as always, Peacey brought the subject round to marriage, particularly in relation to his companion. 'You're not getting any younger,' he would say, or 'Won't you consider finding a wife for yourself?' or 'How we'd all love to see a Mrs Spoons!'

And Mr Spoons, smiling his sweet dimpled smile, would inevitably reply, 'I'll wait and see. That's what I'll do, I'll wait and see.'

This particular afternoon, Peacey, who was blissfully married thanks to Mr Spoons, pressed on. 'Who or what are you waiting *for*?'

he said. 'It's a mystery to me why you can't help yourself like you help the rest of us.'

'Aha,' said Mr Spoons. 'Plumbers always have leaky taps.'

That night, Peacey talked to Mrs Peacey and they agreed that it was time to take matters into their own hands.

'The valley and everyone in it,' said Peacey, 'is as familiar to Spoons as the line of his own eyebrow. If a wife is to be found then I shall have to look further afield.' The following morning, he slipped a note under his neighbour's door to say that he'd been called away on family business. Then off he went in search of a possible bride.

Not having any experience of matchmaking, Peacey had expected a perfect Mrs Spoons to present herself as soon as he left the valley, but he travelled for five days and was disappointed at every stop. On the sixth day, just as he was thinking of giving up, he went into an inn for something to eat and came face to face with quite the loveliest woman, apart from Mrs Peacey of course, that he had ever been rude enough to stare at.

'I'd like a very beautiful meal,' said Peacey, foolishly. 'If you please.'

'Do sit by the fire,' said the voice that matched the face in every particular, 'and I'll bring you some supper.' While he ate, Peacey tried to glean a little information from the people at his table.

'Bella's got a good heart,' said one. 'Been lonely since her husband turned his toes up,' said another. 'Never runs out of ale,' said a third and 'could change sour milk to sweet' said the fourth. Peacey asked if there was a room he could rent for the night and determined to speak with Bella the next day.

Unable to sleep, he went over and over his speech. Being a go-between was a delicate business and he found a new respect for Mr Spoons as he struggled to make the whole adventure sound appealing. After breakfast, finding Bella alone, he told her all about his lonely neighbour and asked if she might consider making the journey back with him. 'We could say that you're my cousin,' said Peacey, improvising. 'Then if the two of you don't get on, nobody will be any the wiser.'

'Goodness me,' said Bella, not quite sure that she understood exactly what Peacey was up to, but curious enough to find out. 'I'd have to ask someone to look after things...'

While Peacey was away, Mr Spoons had made a new friend. A shop in town selling books and fine paintings had been taken over by Miss Esme Dear, a soft-spoken woman who dressed in clothes that seemed to spill from her in frills and flounces. Mr Spoons had taken to visiting the shop as he went about his business, sometimes taking a little box of cakes, sometimes a book or a drawing. They would sit quietly under the green awning and talk as if they'd known each other for years.

'You must let me find you a companion,' said Mr Spoons to Esme.

'I'm happy as I am,' said Esme, who had already lost her heart to Mr Spoons.

Peacey came home triumphantly, with Bella at his side. Mrs Peacey took to her at once. 'We could ask Mr Spoons to supper tonight,' she whispered, even though the walls were thick, 'to meet this dear cousin who's unexpectedly had to come back with you because of family difficulties.'

They sat her in a chair by the window, where the setting sun might most beautifully show off her face. 'I'm oddly shy,' said Bella. 'We might take against each other in the very first minute.'

But of course they didn't. Mr Spoons walked into the kitchen expecting to meet someone who looked like Peacey in a frock. Instead, he stopped dead at the door, forgot to blink, forgot to breathe, and completely forgot his manners.

'This is Bella,' said Mrs Peacey. 'Our cousin.'

'I'm so very pleased to meet you,' said Bella. 'Peacey's told me such nice things.'

The Peaceys ate supper and listened and then they washed up and tried not to listen and all the while Bella and Mr Spoons grew to like each other very much indeed.

'She's not really my cousin,' said Peacey some days later as they sat at tea in the summerhouse. 'I just wanted you to be happy.'

Mr Spoons was so enchanted with Bella that he could only laugh. 'You'll have me out of a job!' he said. 'I never felt so pleased in all my life before.'

At the end of the week, after much discussion, Bella went home and closed the inn. 'I'll go back to dressmaking,' she said to Mr Spoons before she left. 'I never did like all that lifting and cleaning. Wedding dresses are my special favourite.'

'Wedding dresses?' he said nervously, feeling the ghost of a cold wind pass across the tops of his ears.

Bella soon found a cottage in the valley and set about making it into a shop. She painted 'Bella's Brides' on a sign above the window, filled the garden with white flowers and hung little golden bells from a horseshoe on the lintel. Every bride-to-be for miles around came to visit and in no time at all Bella was so busy that she had to employ Mrs Peacey as an assistant.

Mr Spoons found himself with time on his hands. He went to see Esme Dear again. 'Please forgive me for staying away so long,' he said, smiling with his head to one side, dimple uppermost, as he offered her a chocolate cake in a stripey box. They sat in the spring sunshine under the green awning and ate the cake, while Mr Spoons told Esme all about Bella and his extraordinary luck. She choked a little on some crumbs but otherwise their tea passed pleasantly enough.

'I'm dressing the brides,' said Bella to Mr Spoons one day, 'and you're arranging the weddings, so don't you think it would be easier if we worked in the same house?'

The cold wind passed over his ears again, then whistled down his back and settled on his kidneys. He went to see Peacey. 'What am I to do?' he complained. 'She's a lovely woman, lovely in every particular, but I haven't had time to think things through! It's all too sudden.' He stared glumly at the table. 'I wish she wouldn't nag me like that, it makes me anxious, very anxious indeed.'

'You've known her for six months,' said Peacey. 'She's everything you've ever wanted in a wife *and* she loves you. What are you waiting for?'

Mr Spoons was deaf to his friend's good sense. He tried to get on with some work, but after dropping a biscuit tin and losing several cards under the sideboard, he put on his hat and went to visit Esme Dear.

That same afternoon, Bella and Mrs Peacey sat sewing. 'I don't want to upset him,' said Bella through a mouthful of pins. 'It's only been six months.'

'Wait and see, that's his motto,' said Mrs Peacey. 'And we thought he'd wait and see until he was too old to care. That's why Peacey went to find you! If you don't put your foot down it'll be six *years* of "wait and see", you wait and see!'

Bella tacked the last inches of hem and held the dress against her body, turning her head this way and that. 'I'm sure he'll make his mind up soon,' she said. 'And this frock rather suits me, don't you think?'

The last few autumn weddings graced the valley. Bella's garden was russet now, blanketed with falling leaves. The evenings were dark and her conversations with Mr Spoons were less agreeable; there were long silences, awkward moments of indecision and clumsy goodbyes.

Mr Spoons found himself visiting Esme Dear every afternoon, hoping to be soothed. 'I do so enjoy our time together,' he murmured, putting sugar in her tea. 'Your eyes are delphinium blue but here, under the awning, they are green like willow.' Even as he spoke, he surprised himself. He could see her flush behind the napkin she was holding to her cheek.

Esme knew all about Bella but even so she longed to be wooed. 'Oh, goodness me!' she said, putting the napkin under her chin and smiling over it. 'I hardly know what to say!'

Mr Spoons knew that he had taken an irretrievable step. Dizzily, he leaned forward, took Esme's hand and kissed it.

The next few days were most uncomfortable for Mr Spoons. Unable to sleep, he filled out cards for Bella and Esme, drew their faces and tried to see them as he might two strangers applying to him for his matchmaking skills. He walked up and down the garden, thinking, until he gave himself a headache. Finally, he filled out a card in his own name and tried to see himself as he might be seen, noting the good points and the bad. Then he put all three cards in his pocket, waited for dawn and went next door.

'I can't choose!' he said to Peacey, who was half asleep and still in his pyjamas. 'And then there's this all this silly wedding business. I don't want either of them to think badly of me.' He laid the cards out in front of Peacey, with his in the middle and the two women on either side. 'People will say I've been a brute, whatever I do. It's too awful!' He sat down heavily at the table. 'You got me in to this muddle, old friend. Please help me out of it!'

Peacey glanced at the cards. 'We both know what you should do,' he said. 'You don't need advice from me.'

'Indeed not,' said Mr Spoons. 'You're absolutely right. But how are we going to tell her?'

They went to see Esme together and took a very fine cake in a pink box, tied with ribbon. She was waiting by the door as they came in, her hands outstretched. Mr Spoons put the box on the table and bowed. 'How lovely to see you,' he said in his sweetest voice but with his hands firmly at his sides. He weakened momentarily, caught by her smile. 'This is my dear friend, Peacey.'

Mr Spoons was haggard and his voice cracked as he spoke. Esme was all sympathy. She sat him down under the green awning and left Peacey standing rather awkwardly by the door.

'Are you unwell, my dearest?' said Esme. 'You look quite bilious.'

'I thought you should be the first to know,' he mumbled, the dimple only just holding its own. 'After all, I think of you as my *closest* friend and I do so hope we'll always be companions in days to come...' Peacey cleared his throat and Mr Spoons sighed deeply. 'I'm going to ask Bella for her hand in marriage.'

After a long pause Esme stood up. 'My heart is broken,' she said, too quietly for Mr Spoons to hear. She turned her back on them both and started to tidy the bookshelves. 'Congratulations,' she said, more loudly. 'I'm sure you'll be very happy.'

'Dear friend,' said Mr Spoons. 'Thank you.'

Then they went to see Bella who was sweeping her path free of leaves. 'Hello, Peacey!' she said. 'I'm just tidying up before I go.'

'Go where?' said Peacey and Mr Spoons together.

'I'm leaving the valley. There's nothing to keep me here.' She held out her hand to Peacey, said 'Goodbye, Spoons,' and walked back to the house, wiping a speck of dust from her eye.

'Aren't you going to tell her?' said Peacey.

'Actually, I have to say I'm rather relieved,' said Mr Spoons. 'I think I fancy a cup of tea.'

The Peaceys lost interest after that. They were soon to have a baby and even though Mr Spoons dropped in from time to time they never mentioned Bella and neither did he. If anybody asked him why the dressmaker had left her cottage, he would smile sweetly and say 'I think it was a family matter.' Esme sold her shop to the grocer next door who used it as a storeroom; the green awning ripped in a gale and was taken down and sewn into sacks.

In no time at all, Mr Spoons was lonely. Spring was always busy and there were marriages to arrange but he found no pleasure in his work and soon began to lose the best of his good looks.

'You're rather unappealing,' he said to the mirror one morning. 'And I, for one, take no pleasure in your company.' Slumping miserably at the desk, he started to draw on an empty card, first one line and then another until, to his great surprise, he was staring dumbly at Bella's face. Within the hour he was on the road out of the valley.

She was in her new shop, unwinding a bale of cloth and standing in a great pile of white silk, robed like a bride. 'Hello, Spoons,' she said, smiling. 'Do sit down.'

'I hardly know what to say,' he said. 'I've been a fool and it may be too late but I do believe I've come to my senses at last. Bella, most darling Bella, will you marry me?'

Stepping out of the silk, she came to him and held him close. 'Perhaps I ought to wait and see,' she said.

'Perhaps you ought,' said Mr Spoons. 'On the other hand...'

Scorpio Absalee

bsalee was at work in the basement, grating black bark onto a pulpy stew. As the concoction, ruby-rich as blood, came noisily to the boil, red beads spat into the air, scalding her skin. The stew turned to syrup. The potion was ready for the spell. Following the book to the letter, she sang out the words but at the very moment of turning, the red syrup refused her, clotting into a lump of hideous grey gristle that smelt of old meat and rattled in the bowl. 'No!' shouted Absalee. 'Not *again!*' And she emptied the thing into a bucket where it hissed and spluttered.

When Absalee was two her mother, Mara, had shown her how to make cabbage taste like strawberry icing. When she was six she could grow flowers on the palms of her hands and tell her shoes to lace themselves and by her ninth birthday, she was using a crystal for far sight. But Absalee was wilful and proud and although she was very good at magic, she was often careless with people's feelings. Her friends grew scared of her and soon ran off to play with people they could trust. She was no more thoughtful at home, playing tricks on her mother and shape-changing the animals in the yard. 'Did I teach you too soon?' Mara would say, and 'Did I not teach you to be kind?'

Then with no warning, just as Absalee was bursting out of her childhood, her mother began to wither and dry out, like an old apple forgotten in a bowl. When she saw the change, Absalee called up creatures with ridiculous names and chanted until she was hoarse;

she drew all manner of shapes in coloured inks upon the floor and went for days and nights without food or sleep but still her mother shrivelled and faded away, too ill to leave her bed.

Absalee re-read the spell: every word had been followed to the letter. And the book was infallible, or so she'd been taught. From her earliest memory, it had been central to their magic, more used and useful than any other book they owned. Brightly bound in leather and fastened with two clasps fashioned into snake-heads, it was bordered on every page with vibrant colour and artfully worked so that, when closed, it looked exactly like a decorated wooden box.

From time to time, Absalee's parents had allowed her to consult the book for her own magic, but never, since her father's death, had she approached it without supervision. She walked round the room, chewing on the ends of her hair as she always did when deep in thought. She would have to ask her mother for help.

Mara was awake. Absalee piled the pillows at her back so that she could be comfortable and knelt by the bed with her hand on her mother's boney arm. 'I should have asked you first,' she said. 'But I didn't.'

'Asked me what?'

'You'll be cross.'

'Just tell me.'

So Absalee explained about her secret attempts to finish the spell and how the book had refused her. 'I only want to find a cure for you,' she finished. 'So why won't it let me in?'

'My darling child,' said Mara. 'Sometimes we just have to accept things as they are.'

'But I want to make you well again!'

'Just suppose you could…' Mara took her hand and held it firm. 'Wait here with me while I decide what's best.' She closed her eyes and appeared to doze, although Absalee knew well enough that these times were the very opposite of sleep. 'You must leave me here at dawn,' said Mara at last, opening her eyes, 'and go down to the sea. A sailing boat will be waiting for you and a man standing beside it. Ask him to take you to the island.'

'What island?'

'He'll know. Once you're on the sea you'll have no magic so don't think to speed the boat or move the wind to help you.'

'Why not?'

'Because you're not ready, not yet. On the island there's a path. Follow it and you'll come to stairs carved into the rock face. Climb down to the bottom, to the door.' She stopped, exhausted. When she was able to speak again she pointed to a cupboard by the window. 'There's a key on the top shelf, in a coral pot.'

Absalee found the key and put it safely in her pocket. 'What's behind the door?'

'You'll see soon enough.'

Absalee was out of bed long before sunrise. She wrapped some bread and cheese in a cloth and dressed herself warmly against the cold sea winds.

'I'm leaving now,' she said, waking Mara. 'There's food and water here.'

Mara nodded. 'I forgot to say –'

'Yes?' said Absalee, hoping for more instructions.

'Mind the steps,' said Mara. 'They're very steep.'

The man was waiting, leaning on a mooring post. 'Good day to you!' he said.

'Good day,' said Absalee, hanging back a good ten strides in case the sea decided to pounce and carry her away. 'My mother says you'll take me to the island.'

'Does she now!'

Slowly, she came near. His skin was the colour of twigs and his eyes so blue and shrewd that she found it difficult to hold his gaze. He said nothing more, but helped Absalee on board with a strong hand and showed her to the little cabin. Unsure how she was to pass the time, she sat on the narrow bunk and tried to master her fear of being on the water, even going on deck for a minute or two to watch the sea. But the sight of it, the size of it, was worse than anything she could imagine from the safety of the cabin, so she went back to the bunk and lay down.

After what, for Absalee, were several wretched hours, they reached the island. The sailor showed her to the path, a short way upland from the beach. 'I'll wait for you by the boat,' he said, giving her a lantern. 'You won't lose your way.' A wind was starting to stir the jagged bushes to her right and left. With the shawl held tightly to her shoulders she followed the path until she came to the rock face and the recess that Mara had described. A lattice of snakes was carved into the stone, framing the entrance.

Even though she had no choice, she hesitated. Then, holding the lantern tightly, she made her way down the stairs, steadying herself on the wall and thinking always of Mara. At the bottom, in a cave-like antechamber, she came to an iron door, as tall as two of her and many times as wide. Digging the key from her pocket, she turned it in the lock and pushed hard, wincing as the metal grated against the floor.

She expected to see something inconceivably strange, something that her mother had not wanted to describe. For a moment, she was disappointed. Then she realized that the room in front of her *was* strange: it was identical to the basement at home! The book was here too, on an identical table. Why had she come so far, only to find herself in the same place? Unsure what her next move should be, she walked round the table, chewing the ends of her hair.

The book might hold a clue. She stopped in front of it and tried the clasps: they were stuck fast. Had they been nailed down or were they held by magic? She examined it more closely. This wasn't the book at all! It was a box! But she had no key, and in any case, there was no keyhole.

If in doubt, her parents had always said, go straight to the heart of the matter and stay there; the solution will always present itself. The heart of the matter was Mara. Absalee put her hands flat on the box, closed her eyes and pictured her mother. The clasps trembled and fell open. Holding her breath, Absalee lifted the lid.

The box was empty!

Maddened by this new obstacle, she kicked the table. What was she supposed to do next? Some clue, some secret must be hidden inside. Telling her fingers to hunt, she ran them over the painted wood looking for a bump or an indentation that might open a hidden chamber; but the wood was smooth.

Mara, lying in the dark, held a ball of crystal to her face and saw her daughter in it. 'For you, darling girl,' she whispered. 'Use it well.' Then with all the strength she had remaining, she kissed the crystal and sent it away.

Absalee stood back from the table and glared at the box. There must be something essential to her mother's well being in this room or she would never have been sent to find it. And find it she would, no matter what! She set off for the door, thinking to start on the shelves and work her way round but before she'd gone two steps, the air about her shivered and became thick with sparks. Absalee spun on her heel, guarding against whatever had found her there. The sparks dispersed, the air was still again. And in the box, hanging, as if it had been halted suddenly in flight, was a small ball of the purest crystal.

She called it to her, exhilarated, not questioning its origins but assuming that it had been offered for her use. When it was nestling in her hands she looked deeply into it, expecting to see some means for the making of the remedy. At first the ball showed only veiled images, too indistinct to be read, but as her far sight grew stronger, she began to see shadow and light and then a strip of white... a sheet... a bed... a dark room... and her mother lying with her hands crossed over her heart, as still as death.

Shoving the crystal into her pocket and grabbing the lantern, she dashed up the stairs and out to the path. The wind was wild now and she pushed against it, dropping the lantern when the flame went out and conjuring a light to follow in its place.

The sailor was waiting for her halfway up the beach. She ran to him, shouting and waving, but the weather swallowed her voice and made her deaf to his. When she reached his side she grabbed at his shoulder. 'My mother's dying!' she yelled into his ear, 'We've got to go now! *Do as I tell you!*' Without waiting for an answer, she struggled over the heavy sand and braved the boiling tide to reach the boat, assuming that he was close behind. But he'd stayed where he was, watching her. She charged back up to face him, beating his chest with her hands and kicking him in the leg.

'We'll go when I say,' shouted the sailor. 'Understand that.' A sharp, heavy rain began to fall, drenching them both to the skin.

'But I want you to do what *I* say!' wailed Absalee. She lifted her wet face to the sky and began to chant and make strange patterns with her fingers. The rain stopped. The wind died away. Deaf to the sea roaring at her back, she grinned at him, triumphant in her magic.

The sailor pointed over her shoulder. 'Turn round, Absalee.' A wall of weather was rising to the heavens, dividing land and sea for the length of the shoreline. On land all was peaceful but beyond the shivering boundary the storm raged over the water, untouched by the spell.

'Help me,' said Absalee, defeated. 'I must get back to her.' The tide was rising quickly now and the storm coming closer with every wave. As the water rushed in, it pulled at the boat, dragging it off the sand.

'It's time,' shouted the sailor, catching at her sleeve as he ran down the beach. They struggled through the sea and scrambled on board with the spray blinding them and the wind deafening them and the rise and fall of the boat knocking them over and picking them up again. The dark water came at her in great slow waves that stank of rotting weed dredged up from the sea floor. She struggled across to the mast, slipping and falling at every step, and clung there, stiff with terror. The sailor appeared through a web of ropes and pulled himself to her side. 'Go to the cabin,' he shouted. 'Tie yourself to something and you'll be safe.'

'No!' she screamed, 'I'll drown!' Even as she spoke, a giant wave swept on to the deck and jerked them both to their knees. As they fell, the sailor caught her by the hand and kept her close by him while the water rolled away, leaving her deafened and breathless. She found the cabin after that and half-fell down to the darkness below, the fear of being trapped not being as great as the fear of being swept out to sea.

It was difficult to stand on the pitching floor in the dark. There was still no magic in her, she was as powerless here as any other sailor at the mercy of a storm. Struggling to keep her balance, she wound her sodden shawl into a rope and lurched round the cabin hoping to find something that might serve as a tying post.

There was a slight movement, a tremor that was almost a noise, buzzing on her skin. Soaked and bruised and wretched as she was, she sensed the change and was immediately wary.

Mara, or some part of her, was at her side. '*Don't be frightened,*' she said. '*I'm still alive, here in my bed.*'

The palest light, no more than a string of fireflies, shone between them, illuminating their faces. The floor of the cabin lay level beneath their feet; the storm had suddenly died away. Up on deck, the sailor smiled to himself and settled down to wait.

'I thought you were dead,' said Absalee. 'Why did you show me that?'

'Why do you think?' said Mara, raising her hand to wipe away Absalee's tears.

'To teach me a lesson?'

'What lesson?'

'I don't know.'

The light flared, dancing over Mara's head. 'Some things can't be changed, darling girl. Some things just have to be met. Do you see?'

A voice quickened in Absalee as the old resolve began to stir. It's not true, the voice said; my magic can save her. I'll find the right spell...

'Ask the sailor to travel home with you, if he's willing,' said Mara.

The cabin was dark again. Absalee was alone.

At first she thought the sailor was asleep, leaning against the mast in the sunshine, but as she approached he opened his eyes and squinted up at her. 'I'd be pleased to,' he said, shading his face with the flat of his hand. 'If *you're* willing.'

She looked out to sea, embarrassed. 'I'm sorry I kicked you.'

He nodded.

'And thank you for keeping me safe.'

He nodded again.

'Will you summon a wind to speed us?' said Absalee, who had understood, at last, that the sailor was Mara's equal.

'I think we'll just trust the boat,' he said. 'Don't you?'

Sagittarius
Jack Fortune

ack Fortune opened the stable door and offered Ninepins a carrot. The horses were well fed, the hay smelt sweet and the morning was bright with the promise of a fast ride but Jack's face was glum. 'We can gallop as fast as we like,' he said to Ninepins. 'But it always ends with the same old journey home.'

As he was reaching for the saddle – a short ride being better than no ride at all – he heard the slow clip-clop of a tired horse coming into the yard: Motzl, the bay mare, and her rider, Tziztl the judge, Jack's dearest friend.

'Good morning!' cried Jack.

'Good morning,' cried Tzitzl. 'We've just left one place and we're on our way to another. So we thought we'd come and see you in between.' He patted Motzl's neck and looked down at Jack from the shadow of his wide-brimmed hat. 'What say you?'

'I'm overjoyed,' said Jack.

Tzitzl dismounted, stretched his back and swivelled his hips, groaning with every move. 'And how are you both?' he said at last, shaking out the skirts of his long coat. 'You and the mighty Ninepins?'

'All's well,' said Jack.

'Nonsense,' said Tzitzl, pulling a handful of olive stones from his pocket. 'I'm hungry. Let's eat and talk.'

Jack took the bay mare to Wilf, the stable hand. 'Rub her down,' he said, as if the boy knew nothing. 'And wipe the mud from her legs…'

'Yes,' said Wilf, who was used to Jack's long lectures.

'... and stable her with Ninepins because she doesn't like...'

'Yes,' said Wilf, trying to keep his eyes open.

'... and give her some hay as she won't have eaten since...'

'Yes, yes,' said Wilf wearily. 'I think I've got the idea.'

Jack and Tzitzl sat in the sunshine with breakfast laid out between them on an upturned box.

'Where have you been?' said Jack.

'A long way,' said Tzitzl. 'From here, that is.'

Jack swung both his feet under the bench and looked away into what would have been the distance but for the high stable wall. 'I know what's over the next hill and even the hill after that but there's always another beyond...' his voice trailed off.

'So many hills,' said Tzitzl. 'Enough's never enough for you. Not if it was every hill in the whole wide world.'

'I've got everything I need,' said Jack. 'And that's the truth.'

Tzitzl shook his head. After travelling the land for many years and ending disputes with the true word of the law, his manner was always blunt. 'There's a-nagging and a-gnawing going on,' he said. 'And it's time you looked further than the end of your nose.'

'Tell me a tale,' said Jack. 'One of your cases.'

'Isn't it time you found a tale for yourself?'

'I can't,' said Jack. And even as he was saying it, he knew that he could and then he knew that he would and all of a sudden, he was very happy. 'Alright!' he said. 'I will then! I'll come with you. Just a little way though, not too far. And not for long.'

'Long enough,' said Tzitzl. 'For whatever has to be done.'

Jack went to tell Wilf who said, 'You mean I've got to look after the stable by myself?'

'You'll manage. I'll only be gone for a week or two. I'll just remind you about the grooming.' Jack sat on a bale of hay and explained everything all over again while Wilf thought about the quiet weeks ahead and cheered silently to himself.

'Thanks,' he said, when Jack had finished. 'I think I've got the idea.'

'I'll be back before you know it,' said Jack.

'Take your time,' said Wilf. 'No need to hurry.'

For the first part of the journey, they rode side by side. Motzl was a wise old horse, unruffled by obstructions and never tempted to go faster than a trot. As they neared the crossroads she slowed to a stop.

'This is where we part company,' said Tzitzl. 'At least my little Motzl seems to think so.' He reached over and took Jack's hand. 'We'll meet some day soon and then you can tell me a tale to make my jaw drop to my knees. Good luck, Jack Fortune.' Tipping his hat, he rode away to the east, his arm held high in farewell.

Jack chose to ride to the west. The sun came up behind him, warming his neck as he scanned the horizon; there was nothing to be seen to right and left but woodland and pasture. Ninepins galloped on, excited to be given free rein but as they rounded a tree-lined bend, he stopped and tossed his head, whinnying with alarm. A cavalcade of caravans had camped at the side of the road and strange animals, different in size and shape to any Jack had ever seen, were tethered and caged amongst them.

A man, tall enough to whitewash a ceiling without a ladder, approached him on thin bendy legs. 'Greetings,' he said. 'It's a fine morning.'

'It is,' answered Jack, craning his neck.

The tall man was joined by a woman wearing a hat like a water barrel. Her smile was spread wide across her face, displaying a great many teeth. She stroked Ninepins and he moved uneasily, disturbed by the size and smell of the creatures in the distance.

'We're a little alarming I expect,' said the man. He bent to take the woman's hand, she reached high to find his and they hobbled away together, leading Jack and Ninepins to a fire crackling by the road. When Jack had met everybody and been shown the animals, he was offered a tiny bed in a long, narrow wagon. 'You're welcome to stay tonight, and indeed for as long as it suits,' said the man. 'We can always use another pair of hands.'

'It suits me well,' said Jack. 'I'll certainly stay.'

Their first stop was a town a day's ride from the crossroads where Jack and Tzitzl had parted. As they filed down the main street, Jack sat proudly in a borrowed suit on a be-ribboned Ninepins and waved at the crowd. 'This might be enough for me,' he said to himself. 'This travelling life!'

He found a way of sleeping in the small bed and he learnt how to groom the creatures but most of all, he loved to be waking in a strange place, not knowing where he'd be by nightfall. A week passed; he rarely thought about home. 'The stable's another life altogether,' he said to the tall man as they sat by the fire, roasting chestnuts. 'It's not like this, the open road.' But even as he spoke, he knew that the nagging, gnawing feeling had come back and the next morning, to loud, affectionate applause from the door of every caravan, Jack and Ninepins set off, promising to return before the year was out.

After a long ride, they stopped for a rest in the shelter of some tall oaks. While Ninepins nibbled at the grass, Jack lay flat on the ground and fell asleep, lulled by birdsong and the warmth of the day. He was startled awake by the rustle of dry leaves and sat up, smothering a cry of wonder.

A band of wild horses had gathered to stare at Ninepins, who was frozen to the spot, staring back. As soon as Jack moved they skittered off, blazing like fireballs in the sunshine, then stopped again a little further into the forest. Moving slowly so as not to frighten them, Jack saddled up and mounted, intending to wait for a cue from the herd, but Ninepins was impatient to be off. For a moment the scene held, then a silent signal shot through the horses and they sprang away.

Racing behind, Ninepins pounded across the forest floor, splashing through shallow rivers, scrambling into gullies, jumping ditches and clearing fallen trees. Jack had to duck and swerve if he was not to be knocked down by branches or swept away by creepers snaking through the air. When Ninepins lost sight of the horses, he would call and they would answer. Sometimes they would wait for him, their ears lifted, ready to run ahead.

Jack saw the marble towers of the city long before they found the road again. Stretching high above the trees, glinting in the sunlight, the domes and spires were grander than anything he had ever seen in his life. 'Look there!' said Jack, trying to stop and enjoy the spectacle. But Ninepins was thirsty and hot and wanted nothing more than to throw Jack and the heavy saddlebags into a ditch so that he could chase his quarry and outrun them, wing-footed.

The race took them ever closer to the open road until, with a final burst of speed, they arrived at a spot with an uninterrupted view of the city wall. The wild horses were already there, drinking at a pool. Ninepins walked into the shallows and made a show of ignoring them; they made an equal show of ignoring him, standing with their heads together and their eyes firmly fixed on the mossy bank. When Ninepins had refreshed himself, he nudged Jack back to the road and in a second, the chase was on again.

At the city wall, the horses could have veered to the right and headed off into the forest but to Jack's surprise they headed straight for the archway and charged through in single file, their tails high. The guard was so astonished that he stood aside and let them all pass without protest.

The city was teeming. As the herd bolted through the arch they crashed into market stalls and sent them flying, streaking the road with colour. With shouts of, 'Stop! Stop!' and 'You're under arrest!' men in dark uniforms blew whistles and ran in pursuit. But away the horses sped, their hooves hammering on the stone streets as Ninepins raced behind. Then they came to a place where the road curved into a great ring with a statue at its centre. The horses strutted round and round, nonchalant now that Ninepins couldn't take the lead. He stopped and walked to the side, snorting and swishing his tail.

One of the men in uniform caught them up. 'What do you know about this?' he shouted, pointing at the ever-circling herd. 'Is this your doing?'

'Not at all,' said Jack, who was tired of the whole business. 'And I'd rather you didn't use that tone of voice with me, if you don't mind.' Before the man could ask him any more questions, Jack rode off. As if to taunt Ninepins, the horses thundered past, knocking down more stalls as they went and shooting through the archway to cheers and curses from the crowd.

Riding through the market, Jack had spotted a stable and he went there now to let Ninepins be fed and watered and to give himself an hour or two to explore the city on foot. 'What are those towers?' he asked the stable hand. 'Is it a palace?'

'It's the university. Up by the Western Gate.' The stable hand waved vaguely at the street. 'Follow your nose, you can't miss it.'

As Jack left the merchants' quarter he found more and more people walking in the same direction as himself. Fragments of conversation came to him: 'Hasn't been here for a year... what a teacher... I was inspired, my dear... quite changed my way of thinking...'

'Excuse me,' he asked a woman who was hurrying to pass him. 'Do you know where everybody's going?'

'Of course I do!' said the woman. 'We're going to see Tzitzl the judge.'

'Tzitzl!' said Jack. 'But he's my friend!'

'Your *friend*?' said the woman, stopping in her tracks. 'Tell me more!' But the crowd separated them and she went one way while he went another, as happy as could be at the thought of seeing his dear Tzitzl again.

The lecture hall was vast, with a rounded ceiling so high that it had its own small clouds. Benches spanned every wall, tier upon tier, all facing a central podium with a rail set around it for the speaker to hold. At a blast from a single trumpet, the crowd fell silent and Tzitzl, magnificent in a long robe, climbed the podium and stood looking about him at the hundreds of expectant faces.

'Hello to you,' he said, just as if he were alone with Jack. 'And what shall we talk about today?'

Jack sat forward with his hands on his knees, revelling in the questions and exhilarated by the answers. Why had Tzitzl never spoken like this in the stable yard? There was no choice now but that he should join these people, study the law and share in their delight every day for the rest of his life! The talk lasted for hours, although the time passed so quickly that Jack wanted it to carry on for twice as long again. At the end, when the audience rose to cheer, Jack made his way to the door to greet Tzitzl as he left the hall.

'My dear Jack!' he said, flapping his robe with pleasure and leading him through the crowd to a private room where they could sit and talk. 'How did you find me here!'

'It was just good luck,' said Jack. 'I didn't know you were so important.'

Tzitzl laughed. 'I like to talk,' he said. 'And how is the nagging and the gnawing since your travels?'

'I want to study in this place,' said Jack. 'That would be enough for me.'

'To study what?'

'To be clever, to teach, to be like you.'

Tzitzl looked at the floor and scratched his chin. 'I hear that when you teach, Wilf sleeps. This is a bad thing. But you could learn to do better.' He put his arm round Jack's shoulders. 'I'll show you.'

'Why can't I be a judge?' asked Jack, petulant as a boy.

'Who stops you?' said Tzitzl. 'I'm only saying what I know.'

'And if the nagging and the gnawing come back?' said Jack. 'What do I do then?'

'Ask Ninepins.'

Jack did stay for a while. He learnt how to teach without making people weary, and then, because he had to practise on someone, he travelled home with Tzitzl at his side and taught him everything that he might ever need to know about horses.

'Why should I be a judge?' said Tzitzl proudly. 'Now I can put up a haynet!' That evening, when all the jobs were done, he looked up at the wide red-indigo sky and said, 'I think perhaps I'll leave tomorrow. Will you come part of the way with me?'

They left at dawn, at a slow, steady pace to please Motzl, and by noon they'd reached the crossroads. Tzitzl pushed his hat back from his face. 'So here we are, Jack Fortune. And what's the next hill for you?'

'I don't know,' said Jack. 'But I'm sure I'll find it.'

'I know you will,' said Tzitzl, laughing. He turned to leave, his hand held high in farewell. 'Good luck!'

When he was no more than a speck in the distance, Jack, who'd been wishing, just a little, that he might have been travelling with him, bent to speak to Ninepins. 'Shall we give Wilf another day in peace?' he said.

And Ninepins, understanding, lifted his tail and broke into a gallop. The forest wasn't far away; they could find the wild horses and still be back by sunset.

Capricorn

Anwen

nwen tucked the duster into her belt and picked up the broom, anxious to have the chores finished before her father came upstairs. This was no ordinary room to clean. Every table, shelf and sliver of wall was crowded with timepieces, some as small as mice and some, like the Lord of the Year and the Lord of the Day, so tall that each laid flat could have accommodated a hundred standing men.

The Lord of the Year was divided into quarters, each corresponding to a season. Bright enamel flowers, particular to their month, twined round the rim as the year progressed, the present season lying always at the very top. Despite its size, it made no noise.

The Lord of the Day was plainly framed, with a tick-tock as loud as a kettle drum. The clock face was white and its hands and numerals severely carved in black.

The pendulum that commanded it was housed in the length of the square tower, the ground floor of which was occupied by Anwen and her father, the Timekeeper. The long winding staircase was easy for her young legs but the old man was finding it more and more difficult to make the climb. She heard him now as he struggled up, pausing and wheezing on every step. She put the broom away and went to meet him at the door.

'All done?' he said, trying to catch his breath.

'Yes, father.'

'Out of my way then. I've got work to do.'

'I'll help, if you tell me what needs doing.'

'You! And a fine old mess we'd all be in. You've got fingers like a bear in mittens.'

Anwen looked down at her slender hands and touched one fingertip lightly against another. 'If you say so, father.'

'It's nearly noon,' said the Timekeeper. 'Go and make lunch. We'll eat in half an hour.'

The kitchen was at the far end of their apartments and she had to run, spoon in hand, to answer a knock at the front door. Reluctant to involve herself in conversation and delay the meal, she made her sternest face and opened the door no more than a crack.

'I'm sorry to bother you,' said old Pewle, the palace secretary, brushing snow from his moustache. 'I expect you're about to eat.'

'Not quite yet,' said Anwen, standing back to let him in.

'I've got a message from the Minister of State.'

She looked apologetically at the stairs. 'I'd offer to tell him for you, but I'd never hear the end of it. You'll have to deliver the message yourself.'

'You father's very unreasonable,' said Pewle. 'Forgive me for speaking out of turn but you just remember: you're a clever girl, whatever he says.'

Compliments unnerved her. She looked at the hall clock to hide her confusion. 'It's nearly noon. You'd better wait halfway, or you'll be deafened by the clarion.'

Pewle laboured up the tower and stopped as the rolling booming pulse began; a thunder of bells given melody by a pealing fanfare playing in major and minor keys at once. A thin thready chime, ringing at many times the speed of its neighbours, brought the whole cacophony to a close as the last of the twelve pulses was struck. Taking his fingers out of his ears, Pewle finished the climb and stuck his head round the door.

'Yes?' said the Timekeeper. 'What is it?'

'I'm here to ask you if spring might be adjacent. The Minister says he's had enough snow.'

'Seventeen days. And while you're here,' the Timekeeper added, consulting a clock embellished with cherubs, 'His baby should be arriving shortly.'

'Thank you,' said Pewle, turning to prepare himself for the long walk down, which he always undertook backwards to save his knees.

After lunch, Anwen washed the dishes and put the vegetable peelings outside for the goats. Her father had spent the meal reading through his morning post and replying where necessary. He gave her the letters. 'Take these to the palace,' he said. 'And don't waste time gossiping.'

The roads were slippery with ice but she walked as quickly as she dared, her hands and feet numb with cold. On the journey out she'd passed two men trying to clear the pavements; now, coming home, she was surprised to find them fast asleep, slumped over mounds of snow. A delivery boy sat motionless on his cart, his eyes shut; a woman who'd been clearing her path was flopped over the spade, dangling like a puppet. Anwen hurried back to tell her father.

He was already at work on the faulty clock. 'Shush, I'm busy,' he said as she tried to explain what she'd seen. Standing as closely as she dared, she watched as he looked into the mechanism, found a loose cog and tightened it. The clock, a favourite of Anwens's, sprang into life. A tiny painted man on the casing bent to pick up a stone from the pile at his feet, moved along the pathway cut out for him and put the stone down, starting a new pile on the opposite side. He stood still for a tick and a tock, then returned to his starting place, picked up another stone and carried it across. When the second pile was complete, he began again, moving all the stones back to their original position...

Outside, the men woke up and stared at each other, surprised.

Pewle came back, his nose blue with cold. 'The Minister's wife has given birth,' he announced. 'You're to come and pay your respects. And wrap up warm,' he added, in an aside to Anwen. 'It's snowing again.'

The formalities were brief, a mere greeting through the doorway. As they walked home from the palace, the Timekeeper took Anwen's arm, but still he slipped and skidded with every step. Approaching the tower, she stopped for a moment and lifted her face to the swooping flakes.

'Come on,' barked her father, pulling her forward. 'I haven't got all day.' The sudden weight upset her balance and she lost her footing. The Timekeeper, left tottering on the ice, lurched heavily onto his knees and dragged her with him to the ground. Anwen tried to stand but found herself trapped by her coat, which had wrapped itself round his legs as he fell groaning onto his side. Pulling carefully, she managed to free herself. 'Don't move,' she said, spreading the coat over him like a blanket. 'Just lie still while I get help.'

When her father was safely in bed, Anwen sent for the doctor. 'I'll bind his knee,' he said. 'And leave you some herbs to help him sleep. There'll be no climbing the stairs for a month or two at least. Keep him quiet until I visit tomorrow.'

'Come on, girl,' said the Timekeeper, as soon as he was alone with Anwen. 'I can't waste time lying about here. There's too much to do.'

'But the doctor says you're to rest!'

'Don't argue with me.' The old man tried to lever himself up then cried out and sank back into the pillows, his teeth chattering with pain. 'I c-c-can't stay here,' he said. 'G-g-get me upstairs!'

There was a drumming at the front door. The Minister of State, having been told about the accident, was concerned about the aftermath. 'How inconvenient,' he said, looming over the bed in his black coat. 'And what's to become of Time during your convalescence?'

'If you could arrange for two strong fellows to carry me,' said the Timekeeper, 'I could go up in a chair until my knee's quite well again.'

'A chair! What an extraordinary idea.' The Minister lifted a formidable eyebrow and glared at Anwen. 'Are you ready to take command?'

'That's up to my father,' she said.

'Well, there we are then.' Assuming the matter to be closed, he produced a small ormolu clock from his pocket as a farewell gift. 'From us all,' he said, handing it to the Timekeeper. 'You keep an eye on that and let your daughter do the rest.'

Anwen brewed up the herbs and took a cupful in to her father. 'That it should come to this,' he said, staring at the ceiling. 'The world turns on that room.'

'I'll manage, really I will.'

'You don't have the first idea. Come to me at six o'clock. And don't be late. I'll have to tell you exactly what to do.'

Anwen went to bed and lay there, shivering. At one minute to six she took her notebook from the shelf and at exactly six o'clock she tapped on her father's door. There was no response. The herbs had done their work; he was sound asleep. In all their life together, she had never before seen him at rest. His head lay flat on the pillow; his hands were locked together over his heart, clutching the ormolu clock. Shyly, never having touched him while he was awake, she kissed him on the forehead. 'Father,' she called softly. 'Father, it's Anwen.' As she tried to bring him round, hope and fear battled in equal measure: hope that he would wake and tell her what to do, fear lest he wake and spoil her chance to prove herself. But even though she spoke into his ear and shook his shoulder and knocked the wooden bedstead quite loudly with a hairbrush, he lay deeply asleep, totally out of her reach.

At half-past six she made her way upstairs, keys in hand, ready to check every clock, adjusting, dusting and winding as she went round the room. The Lord of the Year and the Lord of the Day were always wound last and, insecure again, she stood between them, thinking that her father would probably be awake by now, appalled and angry at her doing this alone.

Pewle's words, said so often that he must really believe them to be true, burst into her thoughts: *You just remember, you're a clever girl.*

The Lord of the Year was first. Two doors flanked the clock face at shoulder height: one black, one white. The black one opened at a touch, revealing a wooden panel with a lock in the centre. She inserted the key and let go, allowing the device to turn it for her with a whirr and a click and a jangle like forks colliding. The white door opened onto a recess filled with a series of overlapping metal plates. Anwen had watched the Timekeeper often enough, now she did as she had seen him do, pushing and tapping the plates in sequence. They began to move, sliding smoothly across each other until a new pattern had formed and the plates came to rest.

She shut the door, told herself that she was doing well and hurried on to the Lord of the Day. It was very nearly time for the noon clarion; she would have to be quick. The keyhole was oddly shaped, with a circular centre and two crooked arms. Anwen turned the key twelve times, finding it more taxing with each rotation. Then, all jobs done, she picked up the ear-muffs and waited, watching as the clock ticked towards noon: twenty, nineteen, eighteen... the second hand was dawdling... faltering...

Sick with fright, she tried to move but there could have been weights in her shoes, so difficult was it to lift her legs. Struggling through the treacly air, she reached the stairs and pulled herself down the banisters to the pendulum; it was flagging, hardly bothering to swing. Slow, so slow... even her tears...

Her father was watching the door, waiting for her. 'What have you done?' he said, his voice a growling drawl.

'I wound the clocks,' said Anwen thickly. 'Don't know....'

'Stupid...' He lifted his fist and straightened the fingers, revealing a tiny key, small enough to fit in a nutshell.

'Where?'

'White door. One turn.'

In an agony of fear and pain, Anwen inched her way back to the Lord of the Year, opened the white door and tried to spot a possible keyhole. In one corner there were rounded metal plates: petals around a deep, dark eye. She hauled the key into the hole and turned it once.

Under her feet, like an animal burrowing its way across the floor, a signal passed between the clocks, re-animating the Lord of the Day. A tick and a tock and then another, and then, deafening her, the noon clarion rumbling into life. Anwen, reprieved, ran back down the stairs.

'It's alright!' she shouted to her father against the clamour of the bells. 'I did it!'

'You nearly had us all dead,' he shouted back. 'How dare you not ask me?'

'You were asleep. I tried to wake you.' She said, standing defiantly at the end of the bed as the clarion died away. 'What was I to do?'

'It's *my* life.' the Timekeeper said. 'I won't give it to you yet.'

Anwen bowed her head. They became aware of a loud knocking at the front door. Keeping her eyes averted from her father, she left the room and went to admit the doctor. A little way behind him, crunching through the snow and waving vigorously, were Pewle and the Minister of State.

'Well, I've never known anything like it,' said the Minister, banging his boots on the doormat. 'Thought we were all for the compost heap. Was that your doing?' he said to Anwen.

'I'm terribly sorry,' she said. 'There was a misunderstanding but we managed to right it. I think father needs to rest now. Perhaps you could come back later?'

'I'm perfectly well,' the Timekeeper shouted. 'Please come in here.' He sat up as best he could and pulled the sheets straight. 'My daughter was ill informed,' he said, 'and I must take responsibility for that. But she did what had to be done and she did it well.'

Pewle came to stand by Anwen. 'You're a clever girl,' he whispered. 'I told you.'

'I insist on being carried upstairs,' said the Timekeeper. 'I have work to do.'

Pewle cleared his throat. 'I'm sure I don't want to retire either,' he said. 'But there's bound to be a time when these old bones can't manage stairs. What then, eh?'

'I agree, what then?' said the doctor. 'I can barely manage them now.'

'I know how much this means to my father,' said Anwen to the Minister of State. 'Could a chair not be arranged for one visit a day?'

'If you think that's best,' said the Minister of State. 'But no more slowing down, please. That gave us all a frightful turn.'

Then the doctor looked at the Timekeeper's knee and gave Anwen more herbs for a poultice while Pewle offered to dust the clocks and was gently refused. Eventually Anwen and her father were left alone. 'I admit,' he said gravely, 'that I'll have to give you the keys one day. But please allow me to make the decision for myself.'

'Of course, father,' said Anwen. 'Now please rest.'

Pewle was waiting for her outside the door. They went into the kitchen and stood by the stove, warming their hands. 'I was frightened, you know.' said Anwen. 'But I did it!'

'And time passes,' said Pewle. 'I can promise you that.'

Aquarius
William Crane

illiam Crane wanted to fly.

As soon as he could climb onto his bed, he started jumping off it, squawking like a crow. When he went to school he drew birds in all his books and by the time he was old enough to think about girls, a thing he hardly ever did, his room was already cluttered with wings glued together from straw and twigs and dried macaroni.

Not one of his friends was interested in jumping with him from the roof, but they all took it in turns to catch him in a big white blanket as he fell, tied to goat-bladder balloons or sacks of dandelion clocks or long canes hung with feathers; with bags puffing out at his ankles and paper windmills on his ears.

William left school a year before he needed to, a handsome, bird-boned young man, no nearer to his dream than he had been as a child leaping from his bed. His parents, who'd done their best to patch up his injuries, decided to step in. 'We'll never get used to it,' said his father, 'seeing you hurtle past the window. It's time you got a job.'

So, much against his wishes, William was apprenticed to the local glassmaker, in the hope that he might make something useful of his life. How he hated being told what to do! It was unbearably hot in the workshop and he had to sweep the floors and stoke the furnace and make tea on the hour. Worst of all, he could only see the sky when he went out into the yard to eat his lunch, which he did every day, even in the rain, lying flat on his back in the dirty straw.

For several months the reluctant William plodded gloomily about with a face as long as a roof ladder, his mind full of wing-weights and tail feathers. He was much too miserable to be curious about the glassmaker's work and thought only of himself and his bad luck. The old man was disappointed. He'd hoped for a more willing apprentice than this grumpy fellow but chose to be patient, there being no other lads to call on. And besides, he was wise enough to see the hint of spirit trapped behind the sour manners.

Then one day, as William passed by the glassmaker's dancing hands, something – a dazzlement in the light, a blink of colour – held him fast. 'Are you ready now?' said the old man, looking at the wonderment on that once-affronted face.

William nodded. 'Can I make a bird?' he said.

William learnt all that the glassmaker could teach him. He still had to stoke the furnace and sweep the floor but now he ran early to the workshop and left long after the old man had gone home. There were many awful days when the glass snapped and shattered and even worse days when everything that he made looked like dough, squat and shapeless in his hands; but one afternoon, when his hands and his heart and his eye all understood each other at once, he made a perfect bird: a sparrow hawk, poised in flight.

The glassmaker was touched at the beauty of it, and the following day he cleared a space in his workshop so that the two of them could work together, friends at last.

And there William stayed, almost content with his new life. As the years passed, his mother died and then his father and finally the old man, who slipped gently away, napping in the yard.

The morning after the funeral, William sat on his bed, alone but for the multitude of glass birds that filled his room. As he stroked the cool slippery feathers of a swan, its wings raised high, he brooded on a remark he'd overheard at the graveside. 'That William,' a woman had whispered loudly to her friend. 'He must have a skin of glass around his heart!'

Should he have shed tears? He examined his mind again and

found a perfectly reasonable regret at his changed circumstances and some small irritation that he should be expected to put on a show of grief to please a stranger. And then and there, sitting on the bed, William decided that he'd had enough of the shop and enough of his old home. He would sell them both and start a new life somewhere else.

He found the perfect spot near the top of a toothy mountain that overlooked the town. The house didn't take long to build; it was really just one huge room that stretched from the east wall to the west and the north to the south with no interruptions between the roof beams and the floor. There was a furnace on the north wall and great squared windows on the other three sides so that he could see the sky wherever he stood. He was indifferent to flowers and had no interest in growing vegetables or fruit; small wigs of yellowing grass, blown quite flat by the wind, served him as a garden. And with a bed, a shelf, a table, a chair, a washroom outside and all the space he needed to make glass, he was almost content.

William's was the only house for many miles and he spoke to no one but his birds, except on market days when he would walk down the mountain and trade a vase or some fragile bowls for the simple things he needed. Sometimes he forgot to take the items to trade, there not always being room in his memory for birds and baubles to sit together. 'Left your wares behind again?' the grocer would say, as she filled his basket and gave him extra bread. And back up the mountain he'd go, by himself, not even knowing that he was lonely.

The bird first appeared one winter morning, flying low over the house. She was as big as an eagle owl, with silver-white plumage and a gleaming blue beak on her not quite owlish face, a shockingly bright presence in the grey sky. William, who was working by the window and happened to be glancing out, shouted with surprise and dropped the greenfinch he was holding, smashing it on the hard floor. Crunching over the glass, he ran outside just as she was swooping in to land on the flagstones by the step.

Close by, she was even more startling: as lustrous as candle light with a wingspan that stretched fully the length of a man. He stopped well short of her and waited, hardly breathing, while she came slowly to rest. Should he speak? Should he wait? She sat calmly, tilting her head as she studied him. Then, just as he was thinking that he really ought to introduce himself, she took off and flew away over the roof.

Disappointed, William ran round to the back of the house but there was no sign of her, not so much as a dot in the distance. Turning on the spot, scanning the sky, he stood there for an hour or more, watching the crowding in of snow-clouds while his eyes watered in the wind.

The next morning he got up early and ran outside. It had snowed while he slept but there were no tracks between the house and the trees. Dressing quickly he went into the spindly forest for wood and hurried home with less than he needed in case she'd come back and was waiting for him on the flagstones. She wasn't. He ate a sour apple and sat by the window, staring out.

For several days he slept even less than usual and only went to market when he'd shaken out the potato sack and found nothing but a few pebbles and some dry earth. He left in the dark, before dawn, and set a glass thrush to welcome the bird if she chose to visit. 'I'll be back by noon,' he said as he made the thrush firm on the icy step. 'Be sure and ask her to wait.' And of course he forgot everything he'd meant to take to market and couldn't remember what it was he'd meant to bring home. Racing back up the mountain with bags strung across his back, he was sure that the bird would be there but the glass thrush stood by herself, her eye as hard as the cold ground. All that day and the next he lay on his trestle bed and let the furnace die down to grey ashes.

On the second night, lying half-awake, he had a vision: the bird had flown to his house and come to rest by the window, wanting him to make her likeness. When he was finished and the glass was cool, she inspected it and then touched his hand with her silver-white wing. He woke with a start to find himself grasping at the mattress.

How could he not have thought of it before!

William jumped out of bed and dressed so quickly that he missed half the buttons on his coat. He almost ran to the wood store, found it empty and took the cart to the forest where he picked up all the broken branches he could see and rushed them back to the house. By late afternoon the furnace was hot again and William started to work on the bird. The curve of her neck was easy, the lie of her wings easier still and in no time at all she was there in front of him, just as he'd first seen her outside the window. He was jubilant. And hungry! There was an old loaf wrapped in straw on the windowsill so he cut a slice and dipped it into a glass of beer. Then he lay down and looked at her until he fell into a long, deep, dreamless sleep.

Every day for a week or more, he made her again: perching, ready for flight, sleeping with her neck rolled into the curve of her wing. And then one afternoon, just as William had found a way to enrich the dark blue glass of her beak, the real bird came back.

He'd quite forgotten her until he opened the door and found her sitting by the step, looking up at him. Reaching for the wall to steady himself, William missed and fell crookedly to his knees, blushing like a sunset and finding his heart to be suddenly bigger and noisier than his chest could bear.

Strutting off, just far enough to be out of his reach, she arranged herself neatly on the flagstones and gazed at him with that curious tilt of her head. William was cramped and uncomfortable but he didn't want to move in case he frightened her and besides, he had the notion that she was talking to him and that he shouldn't interrupt.

'I want to show you something,' he whispered at last, getting cautiously to his feet. He sidled into the house and visited each glass image of her, seeking out the most beautiful and looking always to the door to make sure that she hadn't flown away. After a minute, knowing that he was too jittery to make a proper choice, he picked up the nearest piece, carried it out and set it down in front of her, smiling as if to say, 'See! This is how extraordinary you are!'

The two birds stood together.

His had squabby feathers, a blot of a face and a neck so lumpish that it would have shamed an ape. Appalled and ashamed, he rushed it back inside.

The white bird stood to watch him go. Then she unfolded her wings to their full width and began, very slowly, to beat them backwards and forwards, making a noise like far-away thunder as she pulled and pushed at the air. As the sound reached the glass bird in William's arms, it shuddered, grew warm and then began to squirm and scratch its way free. 'Stop!' William shouted, trying to hold its legs. 'Stop!' But it was flying now, careering round the room and cannoning into windows, trying to escape.

William ran to the door to point the way and saw the white bird taking to the air with a loud cry. All at once there were feathers pushing and bursting from every piece of glass, wings unfolding and crashing into each other and the racket of birdsong as each new beak opened and found its voice. The first to find the door led the others and they flew out in a great stream, making a furious wind as they passed and banging into William's head until he thought he might go mad with the blows and the noise.

The silence was more terrible. All the feathers that had been lost in the tumult floated to the bare floor and settled there; a hat of feathers crowned his hair; his clothes and skin were soft with down. Wiping his face, he went outside, making little clouds with his feet. He was alone. There was a muted sound deep in his body, like a bottle breaking in a blanket. He lifted his face and called to the empty sky, while the skin of glass around his heart cracked open and fell away.

Behind the house, the white bird was waiting. When she heard him call she flew over his head, circling again and again, until he understood and followed, stumbling over stones, not daring to take his eyes from her. In a clear space, surrounded by trees, she paused for a moment while he knelt to catch his breath. Then, brushing his arm with her silver-white feathers, she gave a loud cry of pleasure. In a moment the sky was full of birds, all calling to their old friend in delight.

And with his feet quite firmly on the ground, William Crane, who hadn't understood that he was lonely, greeted his impossible flock and became one with the woodlark and the heron, the parrot and swan, the peewit and cuckoo and wren.

Pisces
Meggie Mary

eggie Mary was alone on the beach, dancing under the sea-blue sky. The day was very warm and the sand was hot so she thought it might be pleasant to stop for a while and cool her feet in the nearest rock pool. Stepping prettily into the water she started to splash about, but was stopped short by a muffled 'Ow!'

She looked into the pool to see what she might have trodden on. A huge, hideous fishy eye was staring up at her, framed by twists of seaweed. Meggie Mary shrieked and ran back to the rocks. After a moment, when nothing seemed to be moving in the water, she edged nervously back in. Now there were two eyes, set wide apart in a very ugly face that seemed to be nearly all mouth. 'Was that you?' she said. 'That noise?'

'You might look where you're going,' whined the fish. 'Treading on me like that. I'm bruised.' He opened his mouth wide, exposing two rows of nasty little teeth.

'I'm terribly sorry,' said Meggie Mary, 'I didn't see you. Why didn't you get out of my way?'

'Because it's my pool,' said the fish, pretending to go to sleep. She waited for a while, but the tide was about to turn and she was eager to carry on dancing. 'Goodbye then, fish,' she called. 'I'll be more careful next time.'

There was a burst of bubbles. 'Big feet...' said the fish.

The following morning she danced to the end of the bay and back again, and came to a stop by the barnacled rocks. 'Hello,' she said, her face right near the surface of the water. 'I hope you're feeling better today.'

'Depends on what you mean by better,' said the fish in his whining way.

'It must be very boring in there. Wouldn't you prefer to be swimming in the open sea?' In her kindness she quite forgot that the sea came every day to the pool.

'I'm alright where I am,' said the fish, snuggling deeper into the seaweed.

'Goodbye, then, fish,' said Meggie Mary. 'I'm sorry I couldn't help you.' Depressed by the conversation, she danced woodenly and went home early, although the day was warm and the sky bright blue.

She avoided the fish for a week but even though she couldn't see his awful face, she kept thinking about his plight. Why was he so ill tempered and unhappy? Meggie Mary knew that she wouldn't feel peaceful until she'd spoken to him again, so she went back to the pool and ran her fingers gently through the water. The fish looked up. 'Now what?'

'I've been thinking,' she said. 'Perhaps I could bring you a treat or read to you or sing you a song. Just to cheer you up.'

'It's hopeless,' said the fish. 'Don't bother.'

'Then tell me what's wrong,' said Meggie Mary. 'I'll do my best to understand.' And something in her voice touched the fish so deeply that he began to cry.

'You can't do anything,' he sobbed. 'Nobody can.'

'Oh, poor, poor fish.' Meggie Mary was so moved by his tears that she began to weep herself.

'I was tricked,' he said at last. 'A fisherman caught me and said I was too small to eat. He threw me in the sea and then when I was bigger he came back for me and I escaped and now I'm hiding here because if I leave I'll be eaten.' He finished in a rush, his eyes bulging.

Something about this story didn't feel quite right to Meggie Mary.

She was still sorry for the fish but, to her surprise, her tears had dried up. 'That's a sad story,' she said briskly. 'Suppose he found you in this pool? I expect that's why you didn't want to talk to me.' The fish nodded. 'I won't let on,' she said. 'Don't you worry.'

For the rest of the day Meggie Mary thought about what the fish had told her. If he really *was* hiding then a beach was a foolish place to be; he'd be much safer lost in the vastness of the ocean. That night, she went back to the rock pool and looked for him in the dark water. 'It's only me,' she whispered. 'I'm sorry to disturb you so late.' The surface of the water was still. 'Please wake up, I want to tell you something.'

There was a slight movement in the seaweed. 'I can hardly sleep with you screeching at me,' said the fish. 'What?'

'I think you should hide in the sea, then you'll be really safe from the fisherman.' There was a long silence. 'Well?' she said at last. 'I've brought my bucket – would you like to get in?'

Lit only by the faintest of moons, the fish stared up at her. 'I haven't told you the whole truth,' he said. 'If I tell you now, will you leave me alone?'

Meggie Mary wasn't a bit surprised. She put the bucket upside down in the water and sat on it with her hands underneath her chin. 'I'm ready. You can start whenever you like.'

'I used to be a *whale*,' whined the fish. 'An enormous whale. I had an ocean to myself and a lot of small fishes to look after.' He squirmed in the water, waving the seaweed from side to side. 'Then I upset a mermaid and she put a spell on me and I had to choose.'

'Choose what?' said Meggie Mary.

'Whether to be a whelk, a shipwreck or an ugly fish trapped in a rock pool.' He gulped. 'And if I ever see her again she might change her mind and then I won't have any life at all.'

Meggie Mary leaned forward on the bucket and gently touched the fish. 'I'm dreadfully sorry,' she said, her voice tender. 'Of course you can't go back to the sea. What can I do to help you?'

'Perhaps you could pass by from time to time. But don't put yourself out.'

So every day, when she might have been dancing, Meggie Mary visited the fish. Sometimes she told him stories and sometimes she listened while he complained about his life and once she tried to dance for him in the water, but she kicked up some sand from the bottom of the pool and it got in his eyes so she had to stop. One morning, when the fish was unusually cheerful, Meggie Mary found herself mentioning his other life as a whale.

'How wonderful it must have been for you,' she said, 'knowing that you were the hugest being in all the seas.'

'I've never been huge,' said the fish, caught off guard. 'I've always been rather thin, actually.' In the distance the tide began to turn; a lone gull cackled overhead.

'A thin whale!' Meggie Mary said, before she could stop herself. 'I've never heard of that!' And a terrible silence slipped between them.

By the time she spoke again, the tide was edging up the beach. 'I'm going home now,' she said. 'And I probably won't come back.' The fish had all but disappeared into the seaweed. Meggie Mary got up and looked down at the water. 'Goodbye then, fish. I'm sorry you couldn't tell me the truth. I hope you cheer up soon.' There was one noisy bubble and then the pool was still.

That night, Meggie Mary sat tearfully at her window and listened to the waves breaking on the bay. Even though the fish had lied to her twice she still felt sorry for him and his poor ugly face. At sunrise, she tiptoed down the stairs and ran along the beach. 'Fish, fish, I didn't mean to leave you,' she called into the pool. 'I'm selfish and unkind.' If the fish was there, he made no noise. Meggie Mary looked deep into the seaweed but could see no sign of him, not even the tiniest little bubble.

'Forgive me, fish. I'll never leave you again, I give you my word.' But no matter how she tried, no matter what she promised, the fish was silent. Heartbroken, Meggie Mary got out of the pool and sat on the rocks, wrapping her feet in the cold, wet folds of her skirt. 'I don't think I'll ever dance again,' she said, half to the fish and half to herself. 'I couldn't bear to be happy, knowing you were sad.'

And there she sat for a very long time, looking out to sea but not seeing anything at all while the tide came rolling up the beach. A tiny wave touched the hem of her skirt; then a bigger, brasher wave came close behind and soaked her legs. Instantly alert, she saw that the bay had all but disappeared: she was marooned! Slipping and sliding with every step, she clambered up the wet rocks to find a safer resting place but the sea was bolder now and the undertow more grasping. Then a wave, larger than all the rest, swung up and pulled her in. Although Meggie Mary knew that she was alone she cried out for help, but her voice was lost in the booming waters.

Down below, wedged tightly between the two rocks that had become his home, the fish was dreaming: Meggie Mary was calling to him, her hands held out in supplication…

Waking with a start, he looked up.

She was bobbing slowly in the current, her blue skirt billowing like a sea anemone. With a great thrust, the fish flung himself away from the rocks and swam towards her. In the moments that it took him to reach her side, his life as a fish came to an end. He put his arms round her body, lifted her face from the water and, gasping for air, heaved her onto the last bare rock, dragging himself up beside her.

Meggie Mary lay limply on the wet stone. 'Thank you,' she said, as soon as she could speak.

'Don't thank me,' said the man. 'You mustn't.' Keeping his face averted, he touched his cheeks with both hands, feeling for his ears and the fleshy part of his nose. Then, very carefully, he stood up. Breathing noisily through his mouth, he flexed his knees and elbows.

'I didn't see you,' said Meggie Mary. 'I thought I was alone.'

'You were,' said the man. 'In a manner of speaking.' He shrugged, lifting his shoulders as if they'd been tied in knots with rough string. 'Why were you in the water?' he said at last, bending his neck a little so that he could see her.

'Because of a sad fish,' said Meggie Mary, squeezing out her hair. 'I was so sorry for him, and for myself, that I didn't see the tide coming in. He's still down there somewhere, snug in his seaweed.' She looked up and found herself staring straight into the man's eyes. They were round and cold and very pale blue. Unable to meet her gaze, he started to get out of the wet jacket that was clinging to his skin, 'Who are you?' said Meggie Mary. 'I mean, who are you *really?*'

'The tide will go out soon,' said the man, tugging away and revealing skin more grey than pink. 'Then you can go home.' He opened and closed his mouth, still unpleasantly full of small sharp teeth. The jacket came off with a wrench, and he threw it aside.

She caught it by the collar and spread it between them on the stone to dry. 'You look just like my fish,' she said, patting the grey-blue silk into place. 'I mean your eyes are the same colour...'

'Oh what's the use!' he cried, flinging himself round and sitting with his back to her. 'It's true! I was your fish. But you've no idea what I've been through. Under water, up a tree, it's all the same. It's all awful.'

'Why don't you tell me the truth,' she said. 'Tell me why you were in the pool. Don't lie to me any more.'

'You'll think I'm weak.'

'I won't.'

'Then you won't believe me,' he said. 'It's a ridiculous story.'

'It can't be more ridiculous than that story about being a whale.'

'It is.'

'Then I can't wait to hear it, ' said Meggie Mary. 'Please tell me everything.'

'My name's Pompano,' said the man. 'And I'm a poet. Well I would have been if anyone had let me.' He glanced at Meggie Mary to see if she was listening properly. 'And I was in love with a wizard's niece and – oh, you really don't want to hear this!'

'Go on!'

'My father wanted me to marry his best friend's daughter. He thought it would be nice for everybody. But Paralala, the wizard's niece, she was angry and she told me that I should choose a bride for myself.'

'Because if you'd really loved her, you wouldn't have thought twice about disobeying your father.'

'Exactly! I know! That's just what she said.' Pompano's face crumpled with misery. 'But I couldn't bear to choose. I couldn't marry either of them. I just lay on my bed and cried. My father was already disappointed because I wanted to be a poet, and then I had to go and spoil his wedding plans as well, and then Paralala...'

'Oh, I know what you're going to say!' Meggie Mary took his hand and held it firmly, even though it felt like a damp sponge. 'She cursed you!'

'She did, she jolly well did! She came to the foot of my bed and threw some old fish bones at the blanket and howled, "May your salt tears become your prison. And there may you stay until you care for another's pain more than you care for your own". The next thing I knew I was in that pool.'

'And if I hadn't nearly died?' said Meggie Mary.

'I'd be there still and always,' said Pompano. 'I suppose I ought to thank you for saving *my* life. Whatever it's worth.' They sat in silence for quite a long time and then Meggie Mary asked him to recite some of his poems and by the time he'd finished, the tide was starting to go out.

'Come on,' she said, holding out her hand to help him off the rocks. 'It's a lovely afternoon.' They walked along the beach, stopping often to brush tiny shells and pebbles from his soft bare feet.

'Where are we going?' he asked.

'I thought you'd want to find your house,' said Meggie Mary, 'and become a proper poet.'

'I don't know where I am,' said Pompano, 'and what's worse, I don't know *when* I am. For all I know I might have been in that pool for a hundred years.' He sat on the sand and shook his head. 'You go. I'll be all right.'

'I'm sure you'd be happier if you tried to find out where you belong. I could help you to look.'

'Paralala might turn me into a grub next time. And then there's my father.' He picked up a handful of sand and watched glumly as it trickled through his fingers.

'You can't just sit on the beach and drown at the next high tide,'

she said. 'Why not start a new life, here? It's only a little village but there's bound to be something you can learn to do.' She smiled encouragingly.

'I'm no good at anything!' he cried, curling into a ball and hiding his face. 'What's the point!'

Meggie Mary wiggled her toes. She felt very much like dancing. 'Thank you for rescuing me,' she said, 'but I'm going now. You can always visit me if you want.' She picked up a shell and knelt in the sand. 'I'm drawing you a map to my house.'

'I always get lost,' said Pompano, who was still in a ball. His hand stole free and searched for hers. She took it gently, not liking its sponginess but wanting to make a kind goodbye.

'You'd better look at the map soon,' she said. Then, while the tide was out, she danced the length of the bay and back again, lifting her arms to the sea-blue sky.

Other Books by The Wessex Astrologer

Patterns of the Past
Karmic Connections
Good Vibrations
The Soulmate Myth: A Dream Come
True or Your Worst Nightmare?
Judy Hall

The Essentials of Vedic Astrology
Lunar Nodes - Crisis and Redemption
Personal Panchanga and the Five
Sources of Light
Komilla Sutton

Astrolocality Astrology
From Here to There
Martin Davis

The Consultation Chart
Introduction to Medical Astrology
Wanda Sellar

The Betz Placidus Table of Houses
Martha Betz

Astrology and Meditation-
The Fearless Contemplation of Change
Greg Bogart

The Book of World Horoscopes
Nicholas Campion

The Moment of Astrology
Geoffrey Cornelius

Life After Grief - An Astrological Guide
to Dealing with Loss
AstroGraphology - The Hidden link
between your Horoscope and your
Handwriting
Darrelyn Gunzburg

The Houses: Temples of the Sky
Deborah Houlding

Through the Looking Glass
The Magic Thread
Richard Idemon

Temperament: Astrology's
Forgotten Key
Dorian Geiseler Greenbaum

Astrology, A Place in Chaos
Star and Planet Combinations
Bernadette Brady

Astrology and the Causes of War
Jamie Macphail

Flirting with the Zodiac
Kim Farnell

The Gods of Change
Howard Sasportas

Astrological Roots:
The Hellenistic Legacy
Joseph Crane

The Art of Forecasting
using Solar Returns
Anthony Louis

Horary Astrology Re-Examined
Barbara Dunn

Living Lilith - Four Dimensions of the
Cosmic Feminine
M. Kelley Hunter

Your Horoscope in Your Hands
Lorna Green

Primary Directions
Martin Gansten

Classical Medical Astrology
Oscar Hofman

The Door Unlocked:
An Astrological Insight into Initiation
*Dolores Ashcroft Nowicki and Stephanie V.
Norris*

Understanding Karmic Complexes:
Evolutionary Astrology and Regression
Therapy
Patricia L. Walsh

www.wessexastrologer.com